Teenage Fathers

Teenage Fathers

Bryan E. Robinson
University of North Carolina
at Charlotte

Foreword by Harriette McAdoo

Lexington Books
D.C. Heath and Company/Lexington, Massachusetts/Toronto

Library of Congress Cataloging-in-Publication Data

Robinson, Bryan E.
  Teenage fathers.

  Includes bibliographies and index.
  1. Adolescent fathers—United States. 2. Adolescent
fathers—United States—Psychology. 3. Adolescent
fathers—Services for—United States. I. Title.
HQ756.R635 1988   362.7′ 96   86-45896
ISBN 0-669-14586-6 (alk. paper)
ISBN 0-669-14587-4 (pbk.: alk. paper)

Published simultaneously in Canada
Printed in the United States of America
Casebound International Standard Book Number: 0-669-14586-6
Paperbound International Standard Book Number: 0-669-14587-4
Library of Congress Catalog Card Number: 86-45896

The paper used in this publication meets the minimum requirements of American National
Standard for Information Sciences—Permanence of Paper for Printed Library Materials,
ANSI Z39.48–1984. ∞™

88 89 90 91 92 8 7 6 5 4 3 2 1

To my sister, Glenda Robinson Loftin, who was a teenage mother and who has been married to her teenage husband and father of her three sons for thirty years.

Table of Contents

Foreword

T eenage Fathers fills a void in the literature on early parenting and forms a companion for the many writings that now exist on the adolescent mother. The need has been so great for a book just like this one, that it is amazing that it is only now that such a book has been produced. This work effectively makes the bridge between empirical research findings, evaluations of programs that have been designed to support young fathers, and the identification of resources that are needed by practitioners.

Despite the national attention that has been paid in the past decade to the seriousness of early pregnancy and parenting outside of marriage, surprisingly little attention has been paid to the other half of the procreation process, the young fathers. The lack of importance that writers and researchers have given to the teenage father is clearly shown in Robinson's critique of the often-quoted major research studies. Many writers did not even mention the fathers and others did not feel fathers were important enough to include in their research designs. Until now the present literature has not provided help for administrators, counselors, parents, or researchers to find out what are the characteristics of young fathers and what efforts are effective in preventing too early parenthood.

There is even a lack of consensus on the definition of *who is a teen father*. Is he a boy 19 years old or younger who gets a young girl pregnant? Or is he a youth in his teens and early twenties who impregnates a young woman? Or is he a man at any age who impregnates a teenage female? All of these definitions are confused in the published research. Research has not been able to isolate the short- or long-term consequences of being a teen father, because age becomes confounded with other salient variables in the literature.

The cultural contexts in which adolescent fathers live are often left out of the studies. Are these babies conceived on a tabula rasa? What is the impact of their race, economic status, religion, or familial values on their procreative activity? Are writers so comfortable in their stereotypes of young fathers and young mothers that they do not even bother to discuss the environment in which new families and family subunits are created? Surely more needs to be done in this area.

Much attention has been paid to the dynamics that lead to too-early pregnancies. Many theoretical, philosophical, and value-based propositions have been presented and are perpetuated on early sexual behavior and conceptions. These propositions were seldom substantiated by empirical data, but these stereotypical images tended to be accepted when they were in agreement with prevailing views. We all know why teenage pregnancies occur. Babies are created because the youth are sexually active. Why are they so active? Simply because sex is pleasurable. That is how Mother Nature designed things to ensure the perpetuation of the species.

The tendency to delay marriage, but not sexual activity, results in the pregnancies outside of marriage. Then why are youth such poor contraceptive users? Because they are young and they think the way youth in all cultures think—immaturely. Teens who become parents think and function in ways that are identical to other teens who did not become parents in their cultural and economic groups. They are often ignorant about their biology related to reproduction. They find it difficult to delay gratification. They have not dealt with the real world and do not really believe that they will get "caught." Pregnancy (as well as drug addiction, alcoholism, and old age) is something that will happen to other people, but not to them. The very simple facts of the immaturity of youth are too often ignored in the explanations that are forwarded to explain the demographic changes within our society. This book effectively debunks many of the prevailing myths about young fathers.

Adolescent pregnancy is a concern for all groups within our society. Patterns of early pregnancy differ in the different racial, social, and economic groups. The pregnancy levels are higher in youth of color, but the trends have been declining for black youth as they have been increasing for white youth. What factors are contributing to these changes?

We know that the consequences are more severe for youth who are poor and unprepared for the world of work. We know that parenthood often is predictive of limited education for both male and female parents. Remaining in school and developing usable job skills will be the most effective approach to preventing the consequences of early pregnancies. We know that youth of color have fewer resources to meet the demands of parenting too early. We know that social service programs are only playing catch-up once an unplanned pregnancy occurs.

What programs of prevention are effective? Several remedial efforts are described and critiqued in this book. Delaying initial sexual encounters should be one goal. However, it is simplistic to expect that a program of encouraging youth to say "no" will be effective. We need to enable each pregnancy to be a planned and a desired pregnancy. We need programs to help young men become aware that the little decisions that they make on a daily basis may result in lifelong consequences to their lives, the lives of their partners, and most importantly, the lives of their unborn children.

The growing pandemic of AIDS, which is spreading more rapidly in teens than in any other heterosexual group, is expected to have an impact on teen parenting. The dissemination of AIDS-related educational materials about sexual activity will enable teens to have access to preventive information related to contraception. The AIDS impact is anticipated to result in trends toward earlier marriages and the maintenance of monogamous sexual relationships. All of these factors may reduce the incidence of teen fatherhood.

When babies *are* born outside of marriage, we seldom are able to find out about the involvement of the fathers. Robinson effectively covers the research findings and the experiences of young men as presented in the literature. One strong feature of this book is that the results of many important studies and evaluations are clearly presented in everyday language. One does not have to wade through masses of statistics to gather the major findings. The vignettes within each chapter poignantly and starkly present the reality of the life of a young man. They often speak louder and clearer than any statistic ever could.

We find that many teen fathers do attempt to maintain contact with their babies and the mothers. They often attempt to stay involved in the childrearing process. Their relationships with the mothers are not fleeting, but are ongoing and involved. However, when an unplanned pregnancy does occur, young fathers may face a bitter wall of frustration in not being able to make the major decisions related to the pregnancy. Their inability to support and protect the unborn child infantilizes the fathers-to-be. Young fathers have limited resources and do lose some control of the lives of their babies.

The pragmatic components of the book enhance its usefulness for a wide audience. Included are well-organized, practical elements that are missing in many books that only cover the research findings: extensive references; educational materials that have been field-tested; the identification of sources for curricula materials; audiovisual resources; professional and lay journals; and the addresses of organizations active in working for teens and as advocates for their families. All of these form a valuable resource for professionals and researchers alike.

—*Harriette Pipes McAdoo*

Acknowledgments

I want to thank a number of people for making this book a reality. Margaret Zusky, editor at Lexington Books, had the interest, foresight, and enthusiasm to get the book off the ground.

My colleagues at the University of North Carolina at Charlotte have been helpful, especially Dr. Bobbie Rowland, who has continued to nourish me with encouragement and steadfast moral support. I also appreciate the administrative support from Dr. Mary Thomas Burke, Chair of the Department of Human Services, and Dr. Harold W. Heller, Dean of the College of Education and Allied Professions. Dr. Robert Barret has been cooperative and encouraging in our collaborative efforts on teenage fathers over the past seven years. I thank him too for exploring pioneer territory and contributing his chapter, "Teenage Fatherhood Revisited." I give special thanks to Marcy Cheek and Melody Bivens for contributing case material for this book. Appreciation also is extended to Richard Banks, Allan Blount, and the other anonymous adult men who shared their past experiences as teen dads.

Finally, I wish to thank Dr. Harriette McAdoo of Howard University, who agreed to read the manuscript and contribute a foreword to this book, and the staff at Lexington Books whose beliefs in this project helped me get the many drafts of this manuscript into print.

Introduction

In my work with teenage fathers over the past seven years, I became aware of the need for a book that helps students and practitioners understand the scope of the adolescent pregnancy problem, particularly as it affects the long-neglected teenage father. What emerged was a handbook, rare in today's market, that presents teenage pregnancy from the young father's perspective—one that addresses questions and concerns of public health workers, nurses, physicians, health educators, counselors and caseworkers, the clergy, school administrators, psychologists, teachers, and students in regard to the male partner.

This book is a synthesis of my work with hundreds of teen dads. It combines scientific knowledge with actual case studies drawn from private clinical practice and from my original research. After surveying the scope of the problem, I examine the myth and reality associated with how young fathers are viewed. I present the hard truths and tragic consequences teenage fathers must endure. Next, I detail the psychological adjustments young fathers must make. I discuss the many barriers confronting social scientists as they have tried to study these young men and suggest what needs to be done next. A special chapter written by my colleague, Dr. Robert Barret, presents original case studies of adult men who fathered children as teenagers. It shows how the early experience of fathering a child can remain a part of a man's life even though since his child's birth he has never or rarely seen the mother and child.

I explore programs designed especially for teenage fathers in many states and make suggestions to help professionals on how they can involve young men in the childbirth and fathering experience. I also discuss what still needs to be done to come to grips with this mounting epidemic that affects 1.1 million adolescents annually. The book concludes with comprehensive resources on teenage fathers for those interested in further reading or study.

This book is an outgrowth of my desire to put the topic of teenage fatherhood in its proper perspective, to dispel the many stereotypes about these young men, and to improve services to them.

This book, although aimed at practitioners, was written also with students in mind. The clear, straightforward language and readable format make this book an excellent supplement at the undergraduate and graduate levels. Special elements giving suggestions for practitioners and resources for working with teenage fathers make it practical and useful for those preparing to enter a wide range of helping professions. It is intended for courses in public health and health education, nursing, social work, counseling, family life, parenting, child development, education, woman's and men's studies, human services, human sexuality, and developmental psychology.

Headings and subheadings are used to help students understand the organization of the book and point out the major concepts. Unfamiliar terms are defined when first used in the text. Practical problems that students will encounter as practitioners are considered along with possible solutions. The format is designed to motivate students, make learning easier, and allow the book to be used either in highly self-directed or teacher-directed courses. The comprehensive listings of audio-visuals, books, journal articles, names of organizations, and educational and curriculum materials, and the descriptions of intervention programs provide a basis for further research and independent study to a wide audience.

The unique combination of scientific knowledge with real-life practical examples engages the student by illustrating the content and bringing it alive. Case studies at the beginning of each chapter and within the text assist students in applying theory and research in actual situations. Cases also serve as springboards for class discussions on health issues, sex and health education, social problems, poverty and socioeconomic factors, reproductive physiology, and family planning, as well as for demonstrations of nursing care, educational intervention, and counseling and social work techniques.

1
The Teenage Father Phenomenon

> Primary consideration should be the welfare of the child; next in importance is the mother; and last is the father. Thus does a mature social orientation mirror the biological facts.
> —Norman Reider (1948, p. 236)

Before

During his girlfriend's pregnancy, 18-year-old Rob said, "I will support my child and mother of the baby because I love and respect her a lot and will do all I can for her and the baby. . . . They are my heart and I really care."

During

I met Dave in the waiting room at the hospital the day after the birth of his son. He had refused to go home, wanting to stay near so he could watch the boy's first hours. "I didn't think I'd feel like this. He's so little and needy and I'm afraid I've really screwed up his life forever. It's hard for me to let them just give him away to some stranger," he said with tears in his eyes, "but I guess I don't have any other choice. He's got a better chance with them than he would ever have with me. I feel like a real jerk!"

After

Seventeen-year-old Carl felt trapped after suddenly realizing, albeit too late, how much babies need in terms of time, money, and patience: "If I'd only known how hard it was going to be, I'd never let this happen," he groaned. "I thought only about the good times, teaching him to talk and to walk, feeding him every now and then. But he cries all the time, and I have to come up with so much money for his things I can't even afford records anymore! I hate my job, and feel like I'll never be able to finish high school!"

These cases are only a few examples I have come across in my work with teenage fathers who openly shared their feelings before, during, and after the birth of their child. The plight of the teenage father has been of personal interest to me since high school. At 17, my best friend swore me to secrecy when he confessed that he had fathered a baby by his 16-year-old girlfriend. I carried that secret for twenty-three years, never telling a soul until now. Of course, during the 1960s, adolescent pregnancy was not as commonplace and, as a taboo topic, certainly was not discussed as openly as it is today. At that time pregnant adolescent girls were frowned upon by society and required, by law, to leave school. The father's identity was usually withheld, and he continued unnoticed to live a life of uninterrupted silence.

Times have changed. The epidemic rise of teenage pregnancy has made it, without doubt, one of the most widely discussed topics in the United States. Although pregnancies among all teenagers have declined in recent years (because of the decline in the numbers of teenage women), pregnancies among unmarried adolescents have risen sharply. This increase is due to a rise in the proportion of young unmarried women who are sexually active. Births to unwed teenagers increased in the decade between 1970 and 1981. Unmarried females between the ages of 15 and 19 gave birth to 190,000 children in 1970 and 259,000 in 1981 (Wulf 1986b). Although birthrates are decreasing all over the world, they are increasing among teenagers between ages 15 and 19 in this country (Ross 1982). Teenage pregnancy rates in the United States are more than two times higher than they are in Canada, England, and France; almost three times higher than they are in Sweden; and seven times higher than they are in the Netherlands (Wulf 1985).

According to the Alan Guttmacher Institute (1982), 7 million teenage males and 5 million teenage females are sexually active at an average age of 16. Adolescent fathers are responsible for a portion of the 1.1 million unintentional teenage pregnancies each year. Of this number, only 17 percent are conceived after marriage. The remaining 22 percent result in out-of-wedlock births, 38 percent terminate in abortions, 10 percent are resolved in marriage of the partners, and 13 percent end in miscarriage (Alan Guttmacher Institute 1982). Adolescent pregnancies account for 46 percent of all out-of-wedlock births and 31 percent of all abortions in the United States.

Contraceptive Behavior

Adolescent sexual activity is beginning at younger and younger ages and use of contraceptives is haphazard (Finkel & Finkel 1983). According to the Carnegie Corporation, premarital sex is a norm for American male adolescents, with 10 million young men between the ages of 14 and 21 being sexually active (Meyer & Russell 1986). National survey results on teenage males in 1979 indicate that 56 percent of 17-year-olds, 66 percent of 18-year-olds, and 77.5 percent of 19-year-olds have experienced sexual intercourse (Zelnik & Kantner 1980). More recent statistics, however, reveal that sexual activity among teenage boys starts much earlier. In some communities, the average

age of first sexual intercourse is 12 years, and more than half of all teenage boys do not use contraception at the time of first intercourse (Meyer & Russell 1986). Two-thirds of sexually active teenagers have never practiced contraception or have used a method inconsistently (Alan Guttmacher Institute 1982).

In my work with teenage fathers I discovered how regularly the boys said they had sexual intercourse before their girlfriends got pregnant. Most of the young fathers never talked about the possibility of pregnancy with their partners and few practiced contraception consistently. I was struck with some of their comments about why they did not use contraception and their lack of understanding of the real causes of pregnancy. Albert, for instance, said, "I didn't think she'd get pregnant because she had such little breasts." Other comments I heard were: "We had a lot of sex and she didn't get pregnant"; "She didn't look like the type [to get pregnant]"; "We only had sex once a week"; or "I didn't think you could get pregnant the first time."

For a large number of teenage males and females, lack of information about sexuality and contraception is a major factor in nonuse, as was true of some of the young fathers I surveyed. Some teenagers believe pregnancy cannot occur because of the male and female's young ages or the infrequency with which they have sexual intercourse (Zelnik, Kantner & Ford 1981). Some do not use contraception because they believe they are protected from pregnancy risks by the time of month they have intercourse. But they are often wrong in their calculations and pregnancy is the consequence. Many teenage males do not know where to get birth control information, do not have easy access to birth control (Zelnik & Shah 1983), or say they are too embarrassed to buy condoms (Meyer & Russell 1986).

But the most common reason for nonuse of contraceptives is that sex among young people is largely irregular and unplanned so that little contraceptive provision is made in advance (Sonenstein 1986; Zelnik, Kantner & Ford 1981). Initially, sexual encounters are so episodic that many teens fail to use contraception or to use reliable methods. Even in a study where 86 percent of the teens knew about contraceptives and 75 percent knew where to obtain them, only 16 percent of adolescents who became pregnant reported using a contraceptive at the time they became pregnant (Landry et al. 1986). Another study revealed that of the 87 percent of sexually active teens who knew where to obtain birth control devices, only 11 percent occasionally used contraception (Smith 1982). These nonusers were surprised when conception actually occurred.

A large percentage of teenage males do not use contraception because planning for sex is too premeditated and it takes the joy and spontaneity out of sexual intimacy (Finkel & Finkel 1975). Emphasis on sexual spontaneity versus planning is believed to be the adolescent's way of reconciling his sexual urges with conventional morality (Needle 1977). The practice of boys carrying condoms or girls carrying diaphragms is a concrete confession that these adolescents think about and plan for sexual activity. Conversely, more unplanned and haphazard approaches to sexual intercourse seem more innocent, less premeditated, and thus less promiscuous.

Another reason for nonuse of contraception among teenage males is the belief that contraception is the female's responsibility (Finkel & Finkel 1975). On the other hand, Sonenstein (1986) notes that female adolescents overrely on teenage males to use condoms and withdrawal—a factor that underscores the importance of the male partner's role in preventing adolescent pregnancy. Other research suggests changing attitudes in the 1980s in which male and female teens perceive contraceptive responsibility as a shared responsibility between both sexes (Clark, Zabin & Hardy 1984; Sheehan, Ostwald & Rothenberger 1986).

· Younger teenagers (14 to 17 years) are at higher risk for pregnancy than older teenagers (18 to 21 years). Recent findings indicate that the youngest group were less likely to have been pregnant, more likely to leave a reproductive health clinic with no method of birth control, and more likely to switch methods (Philliber, Namerow & Jones 1985). When ethnic status is controlled, findings show that white male teens are more inclined to use condoms than either black or Hispanic teens (Finkel & Finkel 1983).

Although European teenagers are as sexually active as American youth, Europeans are more likely to use contraception—a factor that drastically reduces their pregnancy rate. Fewer than one adolescent in twenty in England and one in thirty in Sweden gets pregnant, compared to one in ten in the United States (Meyer & Russell 1986). High school males in the United States are more likely to use contraceptives when they have accurate knowledge of the risks of unprotected coitus and when they perceive birth control as available and convenient (Sonenstein 1986).

More programs are beginning to emphasize easy access for teenagers by informing adolescents how and where to obtain contraceptives to encourage pregnancy prevention. One example is the Male's Place—sponsored by the county health department in Charlotte, North Carolina—which employs teenage males who go into high-risk communities and talk to their peers about male sexual responsibilities, urge them to visit the clinic, and distribute contraceptives when needed. On a broader scale, a national media campaign was launched in 1987 advocating the use of condoms among youth as a widespread precaution against the spread of AIDS.

Why Teens Get Pregnant

Apart from teeangers' notorious resistance to contraceptive practice, many other reasons have been given to explain the dramatic rise in teenage pregnancies. Out-of-wedlock pregnancy no longer carries the shame and humiliation it did during the 1960s because of more liberalized social attitudes towards sex and premarital pregnancy. Consequently, young folks are less inclined to use contraception. Also the youth of today are constantly bombarded with sexuality through advertising, music, motion pictures, and television. The American media tell adolescents that sex is romantic, exciting, and titillating without ever showing the real-life consequences of spontaneous and irresponsible sexual behavior (Jones et al. 1985). Although this social liberalizing trend cannot stand alone as the single cause of adolescent pregnancy, it certainly contributes to a widespread tone of sexual preoccupation. Many of the other explanations for teenage pregnancy place the responsibility squarely on the shoulders of the young father and lack scientific support (I will examine these myths in chapter 2). Although answers are still unclear, there are probably many reasons rather than just one. Reasons that have received empirical substantiation are the developmental explanations, inadequate sex education, and socioeconomic context.

Developmental Explanations

Developmentally, adolescence is a time when a teenager's actions are governed by a way of thinking called "the personal fable" (Hobson, Robinson & Skeen 1983). This egocentric and unrealistic view of the world leads to such conclusions as "It will never happen to me." Teenagers see themselves as immortal and invulnerable. They believe they are immune from such consequences as automobile accidents, death, or becoming involved in unwanted pregnancies. Over and over again I have heard "I never really thought it would happen to her" when teenage fathers describe an unplanned pregnancy with their female partners. Such magical thinking helps teenagers—especially younger teenagers—to convince themselves that they are somehow special and exempt from the conditions under which others must abide. Sonenstein (1986) illustrates another form of the personal fable as when a teenager engaging in intercourse may develop a belief that he or she is sterile if pregnancy does not occur during the first few sexual experiences. Thus, teens who do not think they can get pregnant or impregnate may hold these beliefs as a result of ignorance about conception or as a result of their first sexual contact when pregnancy did not immediately occur.

Involved as they are in the developmental transitions of their lives, they may be fully preoccupied with their own immediate needs of accepting their bodily changes, constructing personal values, and forming identities. As a result, sexual intercourse may be sporadic and lack thoughtful planning (Allen-Meares 1984). These developmental characteristics are coupled with the fact that knowledge of contraception and sexuality required to prevent pregnancies is absent; parents and schools generally have refused to take action in educating youth about sexuality from a young age in a developmentally appropriate way; and our culture insists on abstinence while continually bombarding adolescents with media containing sexual overtones. Many teens become sexually active before they are capable of the rational thought necessary for contraceptive planning. Until teens can think about themselves as sexual beings, they may be developmentally unprepared for responsible contraception (Fisher 1983).

Inadequate Sex Education

Sexually active teens are left largely on their own with few resources to help them make responsible decisions about contraception. Many professionals believe this contributes to ignorance and misinformation about sex and contraception and ultimately to unplanned adolescent pregnancy. The Alan Guttmacher Institute (1982), in fact, recommends that adolescent males and females need to be educated about sex, reproduction, contraception, and the responsibilities of parenthood *before* they become sexually active to prevent unwanted pregnancies. Research culled from the National Longitudinal Survey of Work Experience of Youth indicates that male and female teenagers have first sexual intercourse before they have taken a sex education course (Marsiglio & Mott 1986). Among teenage boys who first had sex at age 15, for instance, only 26 percent had already taken a sex education course, although among 18-year-olds the figure rose to 52 percent. Additional findings indicate that sexually active teenage males do not begin using contraception until anywhere from six months to two years after their first sexual intercourse (Klinman & Sander 1985, Roosa 1984). Thus, sex education and contraceptive use come too late for many adolescent males who have already become involved in a pregnancy.

Although the need for more information about sexuality has been demonstrated, school-based health clinics and sex education programs continue to be controversial (see chapter 8). Recent concerns about AIDS have led health care experts to campaign for earlier and more complete education about all aspects of human sexuality (Barret & Robinson 1987, Robinson & Barret 1987). Still, many communities continue to oppose candid discussions of sex, fearing they will encourage promiscuity and sexual experimentation. An experimental project in Baltimore, Maryland demonstrated that adolescent pregnancy can be reduced by as much as 30 percent after only twenty-eight months of comprehensive sex education (Zabin et al. 1986). In comparison schools where sex education was not introduced, the number of pregnancies continued to rise by 57.6 percent over the same time period. Students who participated in open discussions, lectures, counseling, referrals for contraceptive services at clinics, and other comprehensive sex education services were more likely to delay first-time sexual intercourse to a later age than those adolescents not receiving these services. Many programs, nevertheless, continue to be thwarted by conservative and fundamental religious groups who argue that immoral practices are being encouraged.

Socioeconomic Context

Psychological factors that can lead to sexual intercourse and often unplanned pregnancies include the devastation of living in economically deprived surroundings where hope has long since vanished. Sexual intimacy without regard to future consequences may often be the only antidote to loneliness and alienation the young person knows. A 17-year-old male who does not see much hope for his future might conclude that parenting is one thing at which he can be successful. He may have sex, ignore birth control, and impregnate a female—in the words of Leon Dash, a *Washington Post* reporter—"because they see those actions as ways to keep a relationship alive or escape their own families, or achieve something in a life filled with failure, violence, uncertainty" (Meyer & Russell 1986, p. 5). According to the Children's Defense Fund (1986), minority and low-income teenagers, with fewer opportunities at their doorstep, are at higher risk of repeating the cycle of unwed pregnancy and raising their own children in poverty:

> In a nation where one's worth is judged primarily in three areas—school, work, and family—it is not surprising that teenagers who cannot find a way to succeed in the first two areas find no reason to delay resorting to the third. For many teens who find that other options are limited or nonexistent, parenthood is filling a painful void. (p. 6)

Certain cultural attitudes and behaviors in regard to sexual behavior are recycled within socioeconomic contexts and passed on from one generation to the next. The generation recidivism hypothesis—that the tendency to bear children out of wedlock runs in families and is passed on through permissive attitudes and role models—has received wide acceptance in the adolescent pregnancy literature. Mina-May Robbins and David Lynn (1973) were among the first to detect certain attitudes, that if passed on to children, contribute to a family generational trend of unwed fatherhood. Unwed teenage fathers in their study, compared to adolescent nonfathers, approved of their own children becoming unwed parents, approved of extramarital sex, disapproved of contraceptives, would marry a woman with an illegitimate child by another man, and naively assumed that their children would not be affected by their behavior. Other research suggests that families and friends of teenage fathers have permissive attitudes regarding premarital sexual activity and pregnancy and that their parents respond favorably to the announcement of the pregnancy (Elster & Panzarine 1983b). Data also indicate that adolescent fathers come from environments where adolescent pregnancy is a common and accepted part of the culture, where teenage fatherhood is viewed as minimally disruptive of their lives (Rivara, Sweeny & Henderson 1985), and where young fathers see nothing wrong with having a child out of wedlock (Hendricks 1983).

Numerous investigations found that teenage fathers have many role models for unwed pregnancies. Young fathers were likely to be products of teenage parents themselves (Card 1981; McCoy & Tyler 1985; Rivara, Sweeny & Henderson 1985; Robbins & Lynn 1973), to have a sibling born out of wedlock (Elster & Panzarine 1980; Rivara, Sweeny & Henderson 1985; Robbins & Lynn 1973), or to have a sibling who was an unwed parent (Elster & Panzarine 1980; Hendricks 1980, 1983; Robbins & Lynn 1973).

Determining the Teenage Father Population

The exact number of teenage fathers is unknown because many mothers refuse to identify the father and in the past his age has not been a statistic of common interest. Numerous studies indicate, however, that most males who father children by adolescent mothers are two or three years older than their partners (Brown 1983; McCoy & Tyler 1985; Nakashima & Camp 1984; Rivara 1981; Westney, Cole & Munford 1986). It has been reported, in fact, that the incidence of teenage fatherhood is not as widespread as that of adolescent motherhood, since nearly one-half (47 percent) of the babies born to adolescent females have fathers who are 20 years old or older (Sonenstein 1986).

Sociologist Clark Vincent (1960) compared ages of 201 unwed fathers with the ages of the females they impregnated. He found that 17 percent of the males were seven or more years older, 21 percent were from four to six years older, and 56 percent were within three years of the same age. All told, 94 percent of the fathers were three years or more older than the mother. Pannor, Massarik, and Evans (1971), in their landmark study, found that most unmarried mothers were under the age of 19, whereas fathers were generally older adult men between the ages of 20 and 29. Other reports suggest that most young fathers are in their late teens or early twenties (Leashore 1979; Lorenzi, Klerman & Jekel 1977; Platts 1968).

Age is an important variable in teen father research (see chapter 5). Under what circumstances, for example, do we consider a male a teen father? Is he a teen father if he is in his twenties and impregnates an adolescent female? Do we include adult men who father children by teenage females in our discussions of teenage fathers? Or do we use the teenage years (below age 19) as the cut-off point? Either way, young fathers in their late teens and early twenties are responsible for 1.1 million pregnancies annually. Separating the teen years from the twenties, the numbers are still high. During 1981, for example, there were more than 129,336 live births fathered by males less than 20 years of age (National Center for Health Statistics 1983). This number is probably low since it does not include those teen fathers whose ages were omitted from birth registration forms. It has been suggested by some authorities that one teenage boy in ten to twenty will father a premarital pregnancy (Elster & Panzarine 1983a).

Race and Socioeconomic Differences

The link between a teenager's educational and economic opportunities and his or her decision regarding parenthood is illustrated clearly by the disproportionately high pregnancy rates among our nation's low-income teens, including minority youths. Although teen pregnancy is a national problem affecting all races and all socioeconomic groups, statistics indicate that low-income and minority teens have the highest rates. The Children's Defense Fund (1986) reported that, although black and Hispanic youth account for only 27 percent of this country's adolescent population, they account for about 40 percent of the teenage females who give birth. The number of births per 1,000 unmarried adolescents ages 15 to 19 is more than six times greater among nonwhites than whites (National Center for Health Statistics 1981). In 1979, for example, 13.7 percent of the births to white females occurred among teens between the ages of 15 and 19, whereas among black adolescents the corresponding number was 26.4 percent (National Center for Health Statistics 1981). Disadvantaged teens, whether black, white, or Hispanic, are three to four times more likely to bear children out of wedlock than more advantaged teens.

Research indicates that premarital sex is more common and occurs initially at a younger age among black teens but that white teens who do have premarital sex have more sexual partners (Zelnik, Kantner & Ford 1981). This same study also found that black adolescent females were less likely to use contraception than white adolescent females. Greater sexual activity and less contraception put black girls at greater risk for pregnancy.

Because black and Hispanic males become sexually active at earlier ages, have less access to birth control information, and have fewer social opportunities and alternatives, they are also more likely to become teenage fathers in their earlier teenage years (Finkel & Finkel 1975, Johnson & Staples 1979). Fewer blacks have abortions, fewer marry during their pregnancies, and consequently more premaritally pregnant blacks than whites have illegitimate births (Zelnik, Kantner & Ford 1981).

The Charlotte Teenage Father Study

The original work on teenage fathers that I conducted with my colleague, Dr. Robert Barret, clarified for us many of the questions we had about these young men (Barret & Robinson 1982). The fathers were recruited through three social agencies in Charlotte, North Carolina with adolescent mothers as conduits. We asked expectant adolescent mothers to request that the fathers complete a questionnaire to help us gather more information on this neglected topic. For each returned questionnaire, we compensated fathers and mothers five dollars each for their time.

A total of twenty-six fathers comprised our final sample, and their average age was 18 years. Table 1–1 shows additional demographic information. They were predominatly black, Protestant, first-time fathers who had completed only tenth grade or less. The majority of the males were unemployed or already gainfully employed in blue-collar jobs such as shipping clerk, plastic recycler, or forklift operator. All were making minimum wage. Most of them described their grades in school as average; many reported making D's and F's.

Table 1–1
Demographic Characteristics of the Charlotte Sample

Characteristic	Number	Percentage
Race		
Black	22	85
White	3	11
American Indian	1	4
Religion		
Protestant	12	46
Catholic	2	8
No preference	6	23
No response	6	23
Marital status		
Previously married	2	8
Never married	24	92
Fathering experience		
First-time father	21	81
Second-time father	5	19
Schooling completed		
10th grade or less	13	50
11th grade	4	15
12th grade	6	23
Two years of college	3	12
Church attendance		
Weekly	8	31
Monthly	7	27
Non-attender	11	42

The young males in our study were involved in an ongoing relationship with the mother, not a whimsical, one-time affair. Most fathers said they were having sexual intercourse regularly before pregnancy, one-half of the fathers said the possibility of pregnancy was never discussed, and 38 percent had used no contraception during sex. Many had discussed financial support for mother and baby or the possibility of marriage with their girlfriend's family. Moreover, the majority (92 percent) were highly motivated to participate in some way in the fathering experience—either in naming the child, providing financial support, or both. Most of the fathers (69 percent) said they continued to see or talk to the mother of their child daily or weekly. Box 1–1 further summarizes some of our findings with these young men.

Combating Teenage Pregnancy

Adolescent pregnancy is a devastating public health problem that harms everyone in its wake: the young mother, the father, and the baby. The grandparents do not escape the aftermath unscathed either. Teenage pregnancy and the AIDS outbreak are the toughest health hazards this country will face before we reach the twenty-first century. Their rampant spread has reached epidemic proportions, and neither has solutions appearing on the horizon. Teenage pregnancy, unlike AIDS, is not contagious in the sense of a disease. But, as I mentioned earlier, it can by cyclic and can spread within families and certain socioeconomic communities from one generation to the next. Both epidemics have become targets of national media attention to combat their deleterious forces.

The severe conditions and consequences of teenage pregnancy and parenting prompted an investigation in 1985 by the U.S. House of Representatives Select Committee on Children, Youth, and Families (U.S. Congress 1986). The committee's report, *Teen Pregnancy: What is Being Done? A State-by-State Look,* described the high cost to teenagers, their children, and the government; the inadequacy of basic information at state levels; and significant barriers to improving services. The most serious barriers reported were insufficient education for adolescents and communities, poor coordination of services, inadequate funding, and insufficient data (Walz 1986). The committee concluded that the nation has failed to meet the challenge of teenage pregnancy in any effective or comprehensive manner:

> It is clear . . . that there is no focused approach to solving the complex problems of teen pregnancy at any level of government. The efforts that do exist are too few, [are] uncoordinated, and lack significant support. In short, the system is broken. (Wulf 1986a)

The Children's Defense Fund, approaching adolescent pregnancy from the standpoint of breaking the cycle, launched a five-year national media

Box 1–1
Teenage Fathers Stay in the Picture*

Most people think that teenage fathers' first impulse is to walk away from their parental responsibilities. In books and movies they are portrayed as self-centered ne'er-do-wells, interested only in sexual gratification, who have fleeting, casual relationships with their girlfriends and hit the road at the first hint of pregnancy.

But our research and others' shows that many young men go through the same emotional struggle and confusion that young mothers do. These boys usually know their girlfriends for a year or more and report feelings ranging from affection to love. A growing number are choosing not to abandon their babies.

For about five years, we have been working with young men who are or are about to be parents. In that time, we have seen at least 100 of them. We and others who are trying to understand them see that they differ markedly from the image the public has of them. In one study we conducted with 26 male parents who were between 16 and 21 years old, we found that 22 believed that they had responsibilities toward their girlfriend and baby and 18 saw the mother and child at least once a week.

Teenage fathers often want babies as much as teenage mothers do, for many of the same reasons. A child may be the first thing in their young lives that seems truly theirs. For those performing poorly in school, caring for a baby may be their first tangible accomplishment. For those reared in troubled homes, the infant may be the first human from whom they can receive love. Bill, 18, tells us, "I kept my son as often as I could, and I worked to give money to his mother. Sometimes I knew they just wanted the money, but I was determined to be more of a father than that."

Although they usually don't marry the mother, many young fathers continue dating her during the baby's first years, and most teenage fathers, like Bill, want to help support the mother and baby. They have strong emotional ties with their girlfriends and demonstrate genuine concern for their babies. "I'll take care of them," says 16-year-old Mel. "I'll give money to buy milk for our baby and I'll pay the doctor bills and for other things." Jason, 18, says, "I plan to take care of my baby and my girlfriend and try to give them anything in the world they want."

Teenage fathers who stay in the picture often face unbridled hostility from their girlfriends' families. Nine of our young fathers said that their girlfriends' parents didn't like or didn't speak to them. Steve, 17, tells us, "I know I could've been much more involved in my baby's birth. But I was afraid to admit that I was the father. When people find out you're the one, they try to take you to court and hassle you. I wanted to go to the hospital with her, but I was scared that would only lead to more trouble for both of us. Anyway, her parents really didn't want me hanging around at all."

campaign in 1986 to combat teenage pregnancy. Eight cities were targeted for the first phase, which consisted of television public service announcements, and posters on commuter buses and trains. One poster of a pregnant schoolgirl, holding her school books, was captioned, "Will your child learn to multiply before she learns to subtract?" Another advertisement that depicted a young girl on the right holding her baby on the left read, "The one on the left will finish high school before the one on the right."

The Department of Health and Human Services awarded $1.2 million in grants to communities across the nation in 1986 to fight against teenage pregnancy. Funded under the Adolescent Family Life Program, projects are designed to develop approaches to encourage unmarried teens to postpone sexual activity and to provide family-centered, community-based care for pregnant and parenting teens, their babies and families. Private funding agencies such as the Ford, Rockefeller, Charles Stewart Mott, and Carnegie foundations have donated grants to individuals and groups across the country to support broad-based approaches to adolescent pregnancy prevention.

Conclusion

Teenage males, especially those from low-income and minority groups, are at high risk for becoming fathers at too young an age. The United States, with the largest teen pregnancy population, is waging a war against this epidemic that affects millions of lives every year. There are no simple solutions and no easy answers. Teenagers are not a homogeneous group. They are widely heterogeneous in terms of age; and their social, cultural, and economic backgrounds are so varied that they experience sexual activity, pregnancy, and childbearing in different ways (Meyer & Russell 1986). Experts have come to realize that combating teenage pregnancy means using a wholistic approach to health care and a variety of measures to meet the multivariate needs of this diverse group of young people.

I will discuss the variety of programs and movements aimed at combating teenage pregnancy and their successes and failures in chapter 8. I will focus in particular on those aspects of prevention that encompass teenage fathers. In other chapters I will discuss adolescent pregnancy from the perspective of the father, who is often forgotten in the shuffle of coming to grips with this mounting social problem. We can no longer afford to turn our heads from adolescent males whose hearts and souls are at stake, for they too must be reached if the aforementioned issues and concerns are to be confronted successfully. The first obstacle in this resolve is separating myth from reality, a task researchers have begun to tackle. I will address these findings in the next chapter.

References

Alan Guttmacher Institute. (1982) *Teenage pregnancy: The problem that hasn't gone away.* New York: Alan Guttmacher Institute.

Allen-Meares, P. (1984) Adolescent pregnancy and parenting: The forgotten adolescent father and his parents. *Journal of Social Work & Human Sexuality* 3:27–38.

Baldwin, W., & Cain, V.S. (1980) The children of teenage parents. *Family Planning Perspectives* 12:34–43.

Barret, R.L., & Robinson, B.E. (1982) A descriptive study of teenage expectant fathers. *Family Relations* 31:349–52.

———. (1987) "The role of adolescent fathers in parenting and childrearing." In A.R. Stiffman & R.A. Feldman (eds.), *Advances in adolescent mental health.* Vol. IV, *Childbearing and childrearing.* Greenwich, Conn.: JAI Press.

Brown, S.V. (1983) The commitment and concerns of black adolescent parents. *Social Work Research & Abstracts* 19:27–34.

Caparulo, F., & London, K. (1981) Adolescent fathers: Adolescents first, fathers second. *Issues in Health Care of Women* 3:23–33.

Card, J.J. (1981) Long-term consequences for children of teenage parents. *Demography* 18:137–56.

Card, J. J., & Wise, L.L. (1978) Teenage mothers and teenage fathers: The impact of early childbearing on the parents' personal and professional lives. *Family Planning Perspectives* 10:199–205.

Children's Defense Fund. (1986) The broader challenge of teen pregnancy prevention. *Children's Defense Fund Reports* 8:1, 6, and 8.

Clark, S.D., Zabin, L.S., & Hardy, J.B. (1984) Sex, contraception and parenthood: Experience and attitudes among urban black young men. *Family Planning Perspectives* 16:77–82.

Connolly, L. (1978) Boy fathers. *Human Behavior*:40–43.

de Lissovoy, V. (1973a) Child care by adolescent parents. *Children Today* 2:22–25.

———. (1973b) High school marriages: A longitudinal study. *Journal of Marriage and the Family* 35:245–55.

Earls, F., & Siegel, B. (1980) Precocious fathers. *American Journal of Orthopsychiatry* 50:469–80.

Elster, A.B., & Lamb, M. (1982) Adolescent fathers: A group potentially at risk for parenting failure. *Infant Mental Health Journal* 3:148–55.

Elster, A.B., & Panzarine, S. (1980) Unwed teenage fathers: Emotional and health educational needs. *Journal of Adolescent Health Care* 1:116–20.

Elster, A.B, & Panzarine, S. (1983a) "Adolescent fathers." In E.R. McAnarney (ed.), *Premature adolescent pregnancy and parenthood,* pp. 231–52. New York: Grune & Stratton.

Elster, A.B., & Panzarine, S. (1983b) Teenage fathers: Stresses during gestation and early parenthood. *Clinical Pediatrics* 22:700–703.

Field, T., Widmayer, S.M., Stringer, S., & Ignatoff, E. (1980) Teenage, lower-class black mothers and their preterm infants: An intervention and developmental follow-up. *Child Development* 51:426–36.

Finkel, M., & Finkel, D.J. (1975) Sexual and contraceptive knowledge, attitudes, and behavior of male adolescents. *Family Planning Perspectives* 7:256–60.

———. (1983) Male adolescent sexual behavior, the forgotten partner: A review. *Journal of School Health* 53:544–46.

Fisher, W.A. (1983) "Adolescent contraception: Summary and recommendations." In D. Byrne & W.A. Fisher (eds.), *Adolescents, sex, and contraception*, pp. 273–300. Hillsdale, New Jersey: Lawrence Erlbaum.

Fry, P.S., & Trifiletti, R.J. (1983) Teenage fathers: An exploration of their developmental needs and anxieties and the implications for clinical-social intervention services. *Journal of Psychiatric Treatment and Evaluation* 5:219–27.

Furstenberg, F.F. (1976) *Unplanned parenthood: The social consequences of teenage childbearing.* New York: The Free Press.

Futterman, S., & Livermore, J.B. (1947) Putative fathers. *Journal of Social Casework* 28:174–78.

Gabbard, G.O., & Wolff, J.R. (1977) The unwed pregnant teenager and her male relationship. *The Journal of Reproductive Medicine* 19:137–40.

Harrison, C.E. (1982) "Teenage pregnancy." In D.L. Parron & L. Eisenberg (eds.), *Infants at risk for developmental dysfunction*, pp. 43–55. Washington, D.C.: National Academy Press.

Hendricks, L.E. (1980) Unwed adolescent fathers: Problems they face and their sources of social support. *Adolescence* 15:861–69.

———. (1982) Unmarried black adolescent fathers' attitudes toward abortion, contraception, and sexuality: A preliminary report. *Journal of Adolescent Health Care* 2:199–203.

———. (1983) Suggestions for reaching unmarried black adolescent fathers. *Child Welfare* 62:141–46.

Hendricks, L.E., Howard, C.S., & Caesar, P.O. (1981) Help-seeking behavior among select populations of black unmarried adolescent fathers: Implications for human service agencies. *American Journal of Public Health* 71:733–35.

Hobson, C.F., Robinson, B.E., & Skeen, P. (1983) *Child development and relationships.* New York: Random House.

Howard, M. (1975) "Improving services for young fathers." In *Sharing*. Washington, D.C.: Child Welfare League of America.

Inselberg, R.M. (1962) Marital problems and satisfaction in high school marriages. *Marriage and Family Living* 24:74–77.

Johnson, L.B., & Staples, R.E. (1979) Family planning and the young minority male: A pilot project. *The Family Coordinator* 28:535–43.

Johnson, S. (15 March 1978). Two pioneer programs help unwed teenage fathers cope. *The New York Times*, 54.

Jones, E.F., Forrest, J.D., Goldman, N., Henshaw, S.K., Lincoln, R., Rosoff, J.I., Westoff, C.F., & Wulf, D. (1985) Teenage pregnancy in developed countries: Determinants and policy implications. *Family Planning Perspectives* 17:53–62.

Kasanin, J., & Handschin, S. (1941) Psychodynamic factors in illegitimacy. *American Journal of Orthopsychiatry* 11:66–84.

Kerckhoff, A.C., & Parrow, A.A. (1979) The effect of early marriage on the educational attainment of young men. *Journal of Marriage and the Family* 41:97–107.

Kinard, E.M., & Klerman, L.V. (1980) Teenage parenting and child abuse: Are they related? *American Journal of Orthopsychiatry* 50:481–88.

Klerman, L. (1982) "Teenage parents: A brief review of research." In D.L. Parron & L. Eisenberg (eds.), *Infants at risk for developmental dysfunction*, pp. 125–32. Washington, D.C.: National Academy Press.

Klerman, L.V., & Jekel, J. F. (1973) *School-age mothers: Problems, programs, and policy.* Hamden, Conn.: Shoe String Press.

Klinman, D., & Sander, J. (1985) *Reaching and serving the teenage father.* New York: Bank Street College of Education.

Lamb, M.E., & Elster, A.B. (1985) Adolescent mother-father relationships. *Developmental Psychology* 21:768–73.

Landry, E., Bertrand, J.T., Cherry, F., & Rice, J. (1986) Teen pregnancy in New Orleans: Factors that differentiate teens who deliver, abort, and successfully contracept. *Journal of Youth and Adolescence* 15:259–74.

Leashore, B.R. (1979) Human services and the unmarried father: The forgotten half. *The Family Coordinator* 28:529–34.

Leppert, P.C. (1984) The effect of pregnancy on adolescent growth and development. *Women and Health* 9:2–3, 64–79.

Lorenzi, M.E., Klerman, L.V., & Jekel, J.F. (1977) School-age parents: How permanent a relationship? *Adolescence* 12:13–22.

Marsiglio, W., & Mott, F.L. (1986) The impact of sex education on sexual activity, contraceptive use, and permarital pregnancy among American teenagers. *Family Planning Perspectives* 18:151–61.

McCoy, J.E., & Tyler, F.B. (1985) Selected psychosocial characteristics of black unwed adolescent fathers. *Journal of Adolescent Health Care* 6:12–16.

Meyer, P., & Russell, A. (1986) Adolescent pregnancy: Testing prevention strategies. *Carnegie Quarterly* 31:1–8.

Moore, K.A., & Burt, M.R. (1982) *Private crisis, public cost: Policy perspectives on teenage childbearing.* Washington, D.C.: The Urban Institute.

Nakashima, I.I., & Camp, B.W. (1984) Fathers of infants born to adolescent mothers. *American Journal of Diseases of Children* 138:452–54.

National Center for Health Statistics. (1981) Advance report of final natality statistics, 1979. *Monthly Vital Statistics Report* (DHHS Publication No. PHS 81-1120). Hyattsville, Maryland: Public Health Services.

———. (1983). Advance report of final natality statistics, 1981. *Monthly Vital Statistics Report* (DDHS Publication No. PHS 84-1120). Hyattsville, Maryland: Public Health Services.

Needle, R.H. (1977) Factors affecting contraceptive practices of high school and college-age students. *Journal of School Health* 47:340–45.

Nettleton, C.A., & Cline, D.W. (1975) Dating patterns, sexual relationships and use of contraceptives of 700 unwed mothers during a two-year period following delivery. *Adolescence* 37:45–57.

Nye, F.I., & Lamberts, M.B. (1980) *School-age parenthood: Consequences for babies, mothers, fathers, grandparents, and others.* (Washington State University Cooperative Extension Bulletin 0667) Pullman, Washington: Washington State University.

Pannor, R., & Evans, B.W. (1965) The unmarried father: An integral part of case-work services to the unmarried mother. *Child Welfare* 44:15–20.
——. (1975) The unmarried father revisited. *The Journal of School Health* 45:286–91.
Pannor, R., Massarik, F., & Evans, B. (1971) *The unmarried father: New approaches for helping unmarried young parents.* New York: Springer.
Panzarine, S., & Elster, A.B. (1983) Coping in a group of expectant adolescent fathers: An exploratory study. *Journal of Adolescent Health Care* 4:117–20.
Pauker, J.D. (1971) Fathers of children conceived out of wedlock: Pregnancy, high school, pyschological test results. *Developmental Psychology* 4:215–18.
Philliber, S.G., Namerow, P.B., & Jones, J.E. (1985) Age variation in use of a contraceptive service by adolescents. *Public Health Reports* 100:34–40.
Phipps-Yonas, S. (1980) Teenage pregnancy and motherhood: A review of the literature. *American Journal of Orthopsychiatry* 50:403–31.
Platts, H.K. (1968) A public adoption agency's approach to natural fathers. *Child Welfare* 47:530–37.
Price, L. (1954) *Out of wedlock.* New York: McGraw-Hill.
Redmond, M.A. (1985) Attitudes of adolescent males toward adolescent pregnancy and fatherhood. *Family Relations* 34:337–42.
Reider, N. (1948) The unmarried father. *American Journal of Orthopsychiatry* 18:230–37.
Rivara, F.P. (1981) Teenage pregnancy: The forgotten father. *Developmental Behavioral Pediatrics* 2:141–46.
Rivara, F.P., Sweeney, P.J., & Henderson, B.F. (1985) A study of low socioeconomic status, black teenage fathers and their nonfather peers. *Pediatrics* 75:648–56.
——. (1986) Black teenage fathers: What happens when the child is born? *Pediatrics* 78:151–58.
Robbins, M.B., & Lynn, D.B. (1973) The unwed fathers: Generation recidivism and attitudes about intercourse in California Youth Authority wards. *Journal of Sex Research* 9:334–41.
Robinson, B.E., & Barret, R.L. (1985, December). Teenage fathers. *Psychology Today* 19:66–70.
——. (1986) *The developing father: Emerging roles in contemporary society.* New York: Guilford.
——. (27 May 1987). Myths about adolescent fathers with policy change implications for health care professionals. Paper presented at the Association for the Care of Children's Health 22nd Annual Conference, Halifax, Nova Scotia.
Robinson, B.E., Barret, R.L., & Skeen, P. (1983) Locus of control of unwed adolescent fathers versus adolescent nonfathers. *Perceptual and Motor Skills* 56:397–98.
Roosa, M. (1984) Short-term effects of teenage parenting programs on knowledge and attitudes. *Adolescence* 19:659–666.
Roosa, M.W., Fitzgerald, H.E., & Carlson, N.A. (1982) A comparison of teenage and older mothers: A systems analysis. *Journal of Marriage and the Family* 44:367–77.
Ross, A. (1982) *Teenage mothers, teenage fathers.* New York: Everest House.

Rothstein, A.A. (1978) Adolescent males, fatherhood, and abortion. *Journal of Youth and Adolescence* 7:203–14.

Rus-Eft, D., Sprenger, M., & Beever, H. (1979) Antecedents of adolescent parenthood and consequences at age 30. *The Family Coordinator* 28:173–79.

Scales, P., & Gordon, S. (1979) Preparing today's youth for tomorrow's family. *Journal of the Institute for Family Research and Education* 1:3–7.

Sheehan, M.K., Ostwald, S.K., & Rothenberger, J. (1986) Perceptions of sexual responsibility: Do young men and women agree? *Pediatric Nursing* 12:17–21.

Simkins, L. (1984) Consequences of teenage pregnancy and motherhood. *Adolescence* 19:39–54.

Smith, D.P. (1982) A needs-based curriculum for teenage mothers. *Education* 102:254–57.

Sonenstein, F.L. (1986) "Risking paternity: Sex and contraception among adolescent males." In A.B. Elster & M.E. Lamb (eds.), pp. 31–54. *Adolescent fatherhood.* Hillsdale, New Jersey: Lawrence Erlbaum.

Stengel, R. (9 December 1985) The missing father myth. *Time:*90.

Unger, D.G., & Wandersman, L.P. (1985) Social support and adolescent mothers: Action research contributions to theory and application. *Journal of Social Issues* 41:29–45.

U.S. Congress. (1986) *Teen pregnancy: What is being done? A state-by-state look. A report of the select committee on children, youth, and families. House of Representatives, ninety-ninth Congress, first session together with additional and minority views (December, 1985).* (ED 266 334) Washington, D.C.: U.S. Government Printing Office.

Vaz, R., Smolen, P., & Miller, C. (1983) Adolescent pregnancy: Involvement of the male partner. *Journal of Adolescent Health Care* 4:246–50.

Vincent, C.E. (1956) *Unwed mothers.* New York: The Free Press.

———. (1960) Unmarried fathers and the mores: "Sexual exploiter" as an ex post facto label. *American Sociological Review* 25:40–46.

Walz, G.R. (1986) Teenage pregnancy update. *CAPS Capsule Bulletin No. 4.* Ann Arbor, Michigan: Educational Resources Information Center/Counseling and Personnel Services.

Welcher, D.W. (1982) "The effect of early childbearing on the psychosocial development of adolescent parents." In D.L. Parron & L. Eisenberg (eds.), *Infants at risk for developmental dysfunction,* pp 115–23. Washington, D.C.: National Academy Press.

Westney, O.E., Cole, O.J., & Munford, T.L. (1986) Adolescent unwed prospective fathers: Readiness for fatherhood and behaviors toward the mother and the expected infant. *Adolescence* 21:901–11.

Wulf, D. (1985) Doing something about teenage pregnancy. *Family Planning Perspective* 17:52.

———. (1986a) Select committee says U.S. teenage pregnancy programs are neither effective nor comprehensive. *Family Planning Perspectives* 18:85–86.

———. (1986b) Teenage births decline by 18 percent in decade, but number of children born out of wedlock rises. *Family Planning Perspectives* 18:87–88.

Zabin, L.S., Hirsch, M.B., Smith, E.A., Streett, R., & Hardy, J.B. (1986) Evaluation of a pregnancy prevention program for urban teenagers. *Family Planning Perspectives* 18:119–26.

Zelnik, M., & Kantner, J.F. (1980) Sexual activity, contraceptive use, and pregnancy among metropolitan area teenagers 1971–1979. *Family Planning Perspectives* 12:230–37.

Zelnik, M., Kantner, J.F., & Ford, K. (1981) *Sex and pregnancy in adolescence.* Beverly Hills, Ca.: Sage.

Zelnik, M., & Shah, F.K. (1983) First intercourse among young Americans. *Family Planning Perspectives* 15:64–70.

2
Teenage Fathers: Myths and Realities

> The more insecure the young male is about his masculinity, the more he may be driven to prove his potency to himself or others by demonstrating his ability to impregnate.
> —Group for the Advancement of Psychiatry (1986, p. 30)

Seventeen-year-old Chris said he was surprised, confused, and sort of mad when he found out that his girlfriend was pregnant. His parents and his girlfriend's parents were surprised and shocked too. But he says they were happy after the shock wore off. Still, life has been hard for Chris since marriage to his girlfriend and birth of their baby. "Not enough money and bills—mostly hospital and doctor bills—and working and trying to go to school have been tough," he admits. "Trying to find a good-paying job and pressures at school have made it rough too. Sometimes the responsibility is too much. But having a little toddler running around the house showing off her pictures makes it not so bad."

Chris says the new baby weakened his marriage a bit. "It's not as strong as it was. It was stronger before Wendy was born. I go to school from eight in the morning 'til two in the afternoon. I go to work from three o'clock to eleven at night. Then I come home and go to bed. I hardly ever see my wife."

If he had it to do over again, Chris says he would try to wait a little longer and be more cautious and mature. As for other boys his age, Chris advises, "Wait until you're older and can financially support a wife and kid."

Chris hardly sounds like the stereotype of teenagers who try to escape the responsibility of fatherhood. In my work with teenage fathers I discovered that the stereotypes did not apply in most cases. Asked about their involvement in regard to mother and baby, teenage fathers in my studies expressed strong desires to actively participate as a parent. James, for instance, said, "I look forward to supporting my child and the mother of the baby because I love and respect her a lot and will do all I can for her and the child." Another 18-year-old father, Scott, said, "I want to take care of them because they are special to me and I do love them very much. Not only that, I care because only I am going to be able to take care of them." Other comments were: "I would try the best I could to make their life best for them!" and "I want to stand behind the mother of my child even after the baby is adopted."

I was also impressed with the affection these boys had for their girlfriends and their children and how much they wanted to become involved with their new families. In reading other research in this area, I discovered other family scientists were reporting similar findings to mine and that the young men in my studies were not exceptions. The more I worked in this field of study the more I realized that, although they had no scientific basis, the myths of adolescent fathers continued to overshadow the facts that were emerging from contemporary research. In this chapter I will discuss these myths, trace their historical evolution, and show how contemporary research has disclaimed them.

Myths About Teenage Fathers

Scientific study of adolescent fathers has lagged far behind that of mothers, as has service delivery to these young men. They have been depicted in books and movies as roughnecks, interested primarily in sexual gratification (Robinson & Barret 1987). Those who were concerned (or foolish) enough to stay around often found themselves forced to the altar by the bride's father and his shotgun. These and numerous other myths about teen fathers can be traced to the early writings of the 1940s, when all unwed fathers, regardless of age, were lumped together for analysis and discussion. Influenced by insufficient data, a handful of anecdotal cases, historical stigma, and the media, five commonly held myths were born out of the sociological context in which laws were made and research conducted:

1. Super Stud myth: He is wordly wise and knows more about sex and sexuality than most teenage boys.

2. Don Juan myth: He sexually exploits unsuspecting and helpless adolescent females by taking advantage of them.

3. Macho myth: He feels psychologically inadequate, has no inner control and, unlike other adolescent boys his age, has a psychological need to prove his masculinity. ·

4. Mr. Cool myth: He usually has a fleeting, casual relationship with the young mother and has few emotional feelings about the pregnancy.

5. Phantom Father myth: Absent and rarely involved in the support and rearing of his children, he leaves his partner and offspring to fend for themselves.

Historical Views of Teenage Fathers

A brief look backward in time indicates that clinicians, educators, research-ers, health care workers, human service personnel, and the courts were all guilty to some degree of creating and perpetuating these stereotypes.

The 1940s: Freudian Themes

The war and postwar eras brought increasing numbers of unmarried mothers to social agencies. An Associated Press dispatch from London, dated 9 April 1947, reported that 5,000 children born out of wedlock to servicemen were being sent to the fathers or father's families in the United States (Reider 1948). Consequently, the term *putative fathers* was coined to refer to the men whom, it was assumed, had fathered the child.

During the 1940s, Freudian themes dominated the psychological litera-ture as explanations for the putative father's "unorthodox" behavior. Uncon-scious motives ran the gamut from the need of latent homosexual fathers to prove their heterosexuality, the expression of hostility by sexually insecure men whose wives were infertile, and the acting out of unresolved oedipal fantasies by unwed fathers who had a need to prove their virility (Futterman & Livermore 1947, Kasanin & Handschin 1941, Reider 1948):

> For some men it is apparently insufficient that they can have sexual inter-course; their neurotic need for definite proof can only be satisfied by having a child. The special condition for fulfillment of this need is that they not be married, and thereby escape full responsibility for their wish. (Reider 1948, p. 233)

The Don Juan myth was conceived on the psychiatrist's couch in the 1940s from the sexually exploitive unmarried father "where the man had illusions of being a special sort of individual who was permitted to go about propagating his kind indiscriminately with no sense of responsibility" (Reider 1948, p. 234). One account in particular referred to a patient as a Don Juan whose amorous activities insisted on the absence of contraceptive devices (be-cause it interfered with pleasure), thus forcing the responsibility of pregnan-cies in which he was involved upon the females (Reider 1948).

Clinical case studies portrayed unmarried fathers as pathological—an im-age extrapolated from patients under psychiatric treatment and generalized to unmarried fathers at large. These old Freudian beliefs held on and, as studies of teenage fathers began to emerge, attached themselves to this body of research, where they have continued to cling as stereotypes until today.

The 1950s: Neurotic Personality

Leontine Young, in her book *Out of Wedlock,* gave the public's view of the unmarried father as a neurotic, unscrupulous character—which of course included teenage fathers of the 1950s:

> In short it was more or less taken for granted that he was in any case a pretty worthless character probably without scruples or conscience, from whom little could be expected, and that little to be extracted for the most part only by compulsion. (Young 1954, p. 131)

Young went on to say that society can never know what the unmarried father is really like as a person until the accusing and punitive attitude is replaced. This attitude was perpetuated by social scientists as well as the courts. Adolescent fathers had few rights and little protection under the law. The legal system, reflecting the prevailing social view, usually ruled in favor of the mothers.

That same decade, sociologist Clark Vincent (1956) published a study of thirty-two unwed mothers and fathers. His conclusion, that unmarried males and females derive mutual benefits from the sexual relationship, in some ways helped carry the stereotypes of young fathers into the 1960s. An unwed female, he said, may use sex in order to date, find a husband, and advance in upward mobility, whereas an unmarried man may seek sex to strengthen his masculine ego and self-identity.

The 1960s: Perpetuation of the Stereotype

Despite the Child Welfare League of America's call for services and research on teen fathers at the turn of the 1960s, research on adolescent pregnancy and parenting continued to ignore the young father throughout this decade. Caseworkers in one report believed that unwed fathers had psychosocial problems and that in 85 percent of the cases the sex experience represented an effort to prove masculinity:

> Vista Del Mar social workers are convinced that out-of-wedlock pregnancies result from intrapersonal difficulties, which manifest themselves in ineffective or inappropriate interpersonal relationships; that both unmarried parents in general are faced with intrapersonal and interpersonal difficulties; and that the unmarried father enters into the relationship because of his psychic needs. (Pannor & Evans 1965, p. 56)

The landmark of the 1960s was the well-known Vista Del Mar study, which produced the first book on unmarried fathers in the United States (Pannor, Massarik, & Evans 1971). Sadly though, only a small portion of the unmarried fathers were actually adolescents (twenty-eight out of ninety-six), and it was difficult to separate them from the older adult men who composed the majority of the sample. From the outset the researchers implied stereotypical assumptions about their subjects as irresponsible:

> Although this book deals with the unmarried father and efforts to help him to act in a more responsible way towards the unmarried mother and the child, it is not enough to say to a young father, "Be responsible." (Pannor, Massarik & Evans 1971, p. xi)

Findings from the study also tended to reinforce some of the old myths from the 1940s. Unwed fathers were said to lack social maturity and responsibility, to be undercontrolled and impulsive, to overemphasize personal gain and pleasure, and to have difficulty in forming lasting and meaningful relationships. Still, it was the most comprehensive attempt to date and it set the stage for the first authentic studies of adolescent fathers that were launched in the early 1970s.

The 1970s: A Turning Point

The 1970s marked a major turning point for teenage fathers in terms of legislation and research. The United States Supreme Court, in *Stanley vs. Illinois,* 1972, extended equal protection to single fathers, a ruling that established the right of single fathers to file suits to obtain custody of their children. Before this case, fathers in Illinois—and many other states—who were unmarried had no legal status as parents. The case helped create the first national awareness that all unwed fathers might not be irresponssible and uninvolved. As other cases were presented that challenged this ruling, the court has consistently upheld its original decision.

Subsequent cases further clarified these rights. In *Rothstein vs. Lutheran Social Services,* the rights of alleged fathers to receive notice of adoption proceedings was assured. In *Slavek vs. Convenant Children's Home,* an adoption was ruled invalid because the unwed father had not been notified of the hearing. Today, as a result of these legal rulings, adoption agencies are required to try to locate unwed fathers. Although many of these efforts are limited to obscure legal notices in newspapers, unwed fathers can rely on the courts to establish their paternal rights.

The term *putative* continued to be used as a descriptor of teenage fathers in the research and counseling services of the 1970s (for example, Klerman & Jekel 1977). Usage of such terms helped perpetuate undesirable stereotypes and implied blame and guilt on the young men. According to Earls and Siegel (1980), "the word 'putative' evokes rather untrustworthy and devious qualities in the young men who may be fathers, suggesting that they should be treated as such." (p. 471). One maternity project in particular viewed adolescent fathers as putative and indeed suggested that counseling services be withheld from them unless they were seriously intent on marriage (Lorenzi, Klerman & Jekel 1977).

Still, the literature reflected the breaking down of gender bias among researchers and helping professionals. The first pioneer studies, dealing exclusively with adolescent fathers, were published in 1973, although they are not representative of most teenage fathers of today. De Lissovoy (1973a, 1973b) studied forty-eight white adolescent married couples in a rural setting. Typical adolescent parents of today live in a more urbanized setting, are not married to their partners, and tend to be nonwhite. Robbins and Lynn's (1973) sample consisted of forty-four teenage boys, half of whom had fathered a child. The major problem with the sample was that the boys were wards of the California Youth Authortiy—a biased population from the start—all of whom had been institutionalized for antisocial behavior.

The 1980s: Decade of Progress

Today, social scientists overwhelmingly agree that males involved in adolescent pregnancy are generally nondeliquent and do not represent deviant ends of the spectrum (Rivara 1981). Research on teenage fathers, although still inadequate, has advanced in quality and number with studies directly assessing adolescent fathers and using interviews as well as behavioral measures (see chapter 5). As box 2–1 indicates, research of the 1970s and 1980s disclaimed the five myths and unearthed a totally opposite picture of young fathers as nonexploitive and as uninformed about sex and sexuality as the mother.

Disclaiming the Myths

Ultimately, research may show that some of these myths are true, but as this section demonstrates, no current evidence exists for any of the stereotypes. Studies show that typically throughout the premature pregnancy experience teenage fathers remain involved—either physically or psychologically—and have intimate feelings toward both mother and baby. The educational and economic consequences for the young fathers are severe and often cause anxiety, yet these consequences are not severe enough to characterize the young fathers as psychologically different from their nonfather peers.

Super Stud Myth

It is true that teenage fathers are sexually active earlier and have more frequent and more varied sexual activites than adolescent mothers. Two-thirds of the males in one study were sexually active as early as age 14 (Furstenberg

Box 2–1
Teen Father Profile Before, During, and After Childbirth

Before Childbirth

- Is uninformed about sex and sexuality (Barret & Robinson 1982; Brown 1983; Finkel & Finkel 1975; Howard 1975; Johnson & Staples 1979)
- Does not use contraception or uses it inconsistently (Alan Guttmacher Institute 1982; Barret & Robinson 1982)
- Has difficulty coping with knowledge of pregnancy and shows signs of clinical depression or stress (Elster & Panzarine 1980; Elster & Panzarine 1983b; Fry & Trifiletti 1983; Vaz, Smolen & Miller 1983; Westney, Cole & Munford 1986)
- Shows role conflict over being both an adolescent and a father (Elster & Panzarine 1980; Elster & Panzarine 1983b; Fry & Trifiletti 1983; Robinson & Barret 1985)
- Plans to provide financial support and participate in child care (Barret & Robinson 1982; Fry & Trifiletti 1983; Redmond 1985; Westney, Cole & Munford 1986)

During Childbirth

- Attends some of the mother's clinic visits and/or participates in preparation classes for labor and delivery (85 percent of the sample) (Panzarine & Elster 1983)
- Stays with the mother during labor (66 percent of the sample) and delivery (25 percent of the sample) (Rivara, Sweeney & Henderson 1986)

After Childbirth

- Maintains contact with the mother and baby (Brown 1983; Furstenberg 1976; Gabbard & Wolff 1977; Nettleton & Cline 1975; Rivara, Sweeney & Henderson 1986; Vaz, Smolen & Miller 1983)
- Contributes financially to the care of their child (Furstenberg 1976; Klerman & Jekel, 1973; Lorenzi, Klerman & Jekel 1977; Rivara, Sweeney & Henderson 1986; Vaz, Smolen & Miller 1983)
- Worries about financial responsibilities, education, employment, relationships with partner, and parenting (Brown 1983; Elster & Panzarine 1983b; Hendricks 1980; Hendricks, Howard & Caesar 1981; Rivara, Sweeney & Henderson 1986)
- Drops out of school and gets poor job with low pay (Card & Wise 1978; Kerckhoff & Parrow 1979; Rivara, Sweeney & Henderson 1986; Rus-Eft, Sprenger & Beever 1979)
- Has higher expectations about childrearing than is developmentally appropriate (Caparulo & London 1981; de Lissovoy 1973a; Rivara, Sweeney & Henderson 1986)
- Has an infant who is at risk for prematurity or other health problems (Field et al. 1980; Phipps-Yonas 1980)
- Has an infant who is at higher than average risk for child abuse (Field et al. 1980; Kinard & Klerman 1980)
- Usually doesn't marry the adolescent mother, but if he does, has a marriage that suffers from discord and eventually ends in divorce (Card & Wise, 1978; de Lissovoy 1973b; Furstenberg 1976; Inselberg 1962; Nye & Lamberts 1980; Rus-Eft, Sprenger & Beever 1979)

1976), and in another study 52 percent of the teen fathers had their first sexual intercourse between ages 13 and 14 (Brown 1983). This early sexual activity leads many lay and professional persons to assume that young fathers know more about sexuality and reproduction than they actually do. The fact is, however, that they are as uninformed about sex and sexuality as the young mother and other teenage boys in general (Howard 1975).

Shirley Brown (1983) reported that most of the thirty-three teen fathers and thirty-three teen mothers in her study knew that sexual intercourse could cause pregnancy. Still, less than half knew the most critical time of conception and even fewer knew the more effective methods of birth control. Other data also suggest that two-thirds of sexually active teenagers have either never or inconsistently practiced contraception; 41 percent thought (out of ignorance) that they could not become or get someone pregnant (Alan Guttmacher Institute 1982). In another survey of pregnant teenagers, 62 percent had never used contraception because they thought they were too young to get pregnant, had sex too infrequently, had sex at a time in the month when they thought that they could not become pregnant, could not obtain contraceptives because of availability or cost problems, believed that contraception would interfere with spontaneity or pleasure, had medical or moral objections to contraception, or desired to become pregnant (Moore & Burt 1982). The results of these studies suggest that adolescent fathers lack adequate knowledge of reproductive physiology and indicate their need for more information about human sexuality.

Don Juan Myth

As sociologist Clark Vincent (1960) first pointed out, the label of *sexual exploiter* is frequently affixed to unmarried fathers and is used implicitly as a partial explanation of the cause of illegitimacy:

> It is when pregnancy without marriage occurs that he is labeled the exploiter, she the exploited. His superiority in age, education, and socio-economic status, which would have been viewed as evidence of her desirability and as a rightful reward for her feminine skills if marriage had occurred, is now pointed to as evidence of his exploitative position—of which he took advantage. (p. 45)

In his analysis, however, Vincent maintained that the popular notion of unwed fathers as sexual exploiters of unsophisticated girls was false. Others have more recently emphasized that it is rare that an adolescent male takes sexual advantage of a seemingly helpless adolescent female, since they are within three or four years of age, come from similar socioeconomic backgrounds, have equivalent schooling, and are involved in a meaningful relationship (Elster & Panzarine 1983a).

Shirley Brown (1983), who was interested in the widespread Don Juan explanation for teen pregnancy, asked thirty-three adolescent fathers and mothers to respond to a number of statements relating to sexual exploitation. Overall, Brown found strong disagreement with sexually exploitative language. Nearly all couples (96 percent) disagreed with the notion that it is okay for boys to say "I love you" to his girlfriend so that he can have sex with her. Most couples (82 percent) did not believe that if a guy gets a girl pregnant, it is not his fault because she should have protected herself. Almost three-fourths (71 percent) disagreed that most males think that getting a girl pregnant is evidence of his manhood.

These findings parallel a previous study by Leo Hendricks (1982), who found that ninety-five black teenage fathers in three U.S. cities (Tulsa, Chicago, and Columbus) were similar in their affection and regard for the mother and for the child's future. His results did not support the myth of an exploitative, irresponsible, and uncaring teenage father. The majority disagreed that it is okay to tell a girl that you love her so that you can have sex with her. Most also disagreed with the adage, "getting a girl pregnant proves that you are a man."

Additional data presented by Sonenstein (1986) indicate that most teenage males are not sexual adventurers and do not fit the stereotypical image of young men as promiscuous opportunists. Instead, over half have their first sexual intercourse with someone with whom they are engaged or going steady.

Macho Myth

The macho myth appeared in the early literature when it was suggested that adolescent fathers impregnate young women out of psychological inadequacy and as a means of proving their masculinity. Despite these speculations, empirical research generally shows that adolescent fathers are psychologically and intellectually more alike than different from their nonfather contemporaries (Earls & Siegel 1980, Pauker 1971), a topic that will be discussed in considerable detail in chapter 4. Still, because of their young age, adolescent fathers are usually psychologically ill-prepared for fatherhood. They tend to be ambivalent regarding their readiness to assume the fathering role of provider and caretaker (Rothstein 1978; Westney, Cole & Munford 1986). Although young fathers sometimes undergo depression and emotional turmoil as a natural consequence of their unfortuante circumstances, research has shown that they are psychologically normal (Pauker 1971). Another erroneous belief that is said to make the teenage father psychologically inadequate is his lack of inner control (see box 2–2).

Box 2–2
Teen Fathers Out of Control?

Do adolescent fathers have control over their lives? Or are they bent and swayed at the mercy of their everyday worlds? A common working hypothesis used in the past to explain why some adolescents get pregnant and some do not has been that adolescent fathers, compared to their nonfather agemates, have less control and say-so over their personal lives in general and their sexual urges in particular. This lack of internal control, so the speculation goes, places these young men in the control of external factors such as chance and fate and suggests that teenage males who impregnate their girlfriends have externalized their responsibilities, resigned themselves to their circumstances, and as a consequence do not control their sexual urges.

We wanted to test the validity of this hypothesis with our sample of adolescent fathers in Charlotte, North Carolina (Robinson, Barret & Skeen 1983). We chose those young men who had completed the locus of control measures (an assessment of internal/external control) and who were less than 20 years of age. Ten of the young men either did not complete the forms or were over 20 years old. But twenty adolescents, with an average age of 17.5, met our criteria. We gave the same test to another group of twenty adolescent nonfathers, matched by age with the fathers, from the Big Stone Gap Public School System in Virginia. The Virginia adolescents, with an average age of 17.2, came from intact, middle-income families, and their parents worked in blue collar or professional jobs.

We found that the teenage fathers felt as much in control of their lives as the identical-aged group of male adolescents from Virginia who had never fathered a child. Having found no differences, we decided to go a step further. We took a closer look at the twelve older unwed fathers in our original sample (with an average age of 21.4 years) who had not met the age criterion for inclusion in the teenage father analysis. We randomly selected twelve teenage fathers to compare with the adult fathers. Despite an age difference of almost four years, we found that the adolescent fathers felt equally in control of their lives, compared to the adult fathers.

Our findings on fate control compare favorably with other studies of unwed adolescent mothers and fathers. One investigation in particular showed unwed adolescent mothers (age 16.1) to feel as much in control of their fate as adolescent females (age 16.1) who were not mothers (Silk 1981). Our findings were also similar to those of Leo Hendricks (1980), who studied twenty adolescent fathers in Tulsa, Oklahoma and discovered that 80 percent felt that what happens to them is of their own doing and that their destiny is not governed by chance, fate, or by other people. A third study confirmed that adolescent fathers show no differences from their nonfather peers in their sense of personal control and responsibility for their own lives (McCoy & Tyler 1985).

On the basis of our data and other recent studies, we must conclude that lack of inner control does not explain the high incidence of adolescent fatherhood. In fact, teenage fathers appear to be as much in control of their lives as their agemates who have not fathered children and as older men who have fathered children out of wedlock.

Mr. Cool Myth

One of the most prominent myths about teenage fathers is that their relationships with the mothers are cool and casual. Even in situations where the unwed father makes provisions, his actions can be easily explained away: "He may be quite ready to contribute to the care of the child since he had a certain fondness for the girl, although it was nothing but a casual relationship (Reider 1948, p. 235).

But more contemporary research suggests that teenage fathers have close ties with their girlfriends. Usually, the couple has known each other for at least a year, and their feelings range from affection to love (Brown 1983, Hendricks 1983, Howard 1975). One group of researchers, in fact, reported that over half of the adolescent mothers and fathers in their study attended the same school, and more than 67 percent of them had been friends from one to four years prior to pregnancy (Westney, Cole & Munford 1986). Another investigation (Brown 1983) found that, contrary to beliefs that teen mothers are committed and teen fathers are casual about intimate relationships, adolescent couples share a perception of affection. Findings showed that teenage partners whose affections are mutual not only feel their relationships to be stable but also are serious enough to consider marriage.

The relationships described by the adolescent fathers in my own studies are close and caring, as the opening cases illustrate (Barret & Robinson 1987, Robinson & Barret 1986). Although wanting to remain unmarried, most of the fathers in these studies had strong emotional ties to their pregnant girlfriends. Hendricks (1980) also found teenage fathers to be willing to provide emotional and financial support while also recognizing the hurdles of inadequate education, money, and emotional resources. Such feeling-oriented comments stand in stark contrast to the stereotype of the teenage father as irresponsible and uncaring. Caseworkers also verify adolescent fathers' interest in the mothers and babies and their desires to be active fathers (Pannor & Evans 1975).

Phantom Father Myth

Teenage fathers have been traditionally characterized as missing or difficult to locate. One early account portrays the unmarried father as a phantom, whose existence is elusive or visionary: "Often the man will leave town or the state so that legal action will be more difficult, but will continue to send some small sum of money, thus salving his conscience" (Reider 1948, p. 235).

Numerous investigations, however, indicate the young father's desire to participate in pregnancy, parenthood, and childrearing. In one study, 91 percent of the adolescent males said they would provide financial support and

87 percent wanted to participate in child care (Redmond 1985). In another study, 96 percent of the unwed, expectant fathers said they planned to maintain close contact with the mother, to interact socially with the baby, and to help with the infant's physical care (Westney, Cole & Munford 1986). In still another report, the majority of teen fathers were interested in understanding what will happen during the birth of their baby (69 percent) and how to take better care of the baby after birth (81 percent) (Elster & Panzarine 1983b). Out of the twenty adolescent father volunteers interviewed by Panzarine and Elster (1983), most were actively involved in the pregnancy. The researchers found that seventeen attended at least some of their partner's clinic visits and/or participated in preparatory classes for labor and delivery. Only three fathers expressed any negative feelings about either fatherhood or the baby. Two-thirds of the eighty-one teenage fathers in another study stayed with the mother during labor, 25 percent were in the delivery room, and 88 percent visited their children in the nursery (Rivara, Sweeney & Henderson 1986).

Gabbard and Wolff (1977) reported that 53 percent of the married teen fathers in their sample maintained regular and frequent contact and 84 percent had continuous contact of at least some regularity throughout the pregnancy. Klerman and Jekel (1973) also found that two-thirds of the fathers they studied contributed at least something to support both mother and child. Vaz, Smolen, and Miller (1983) reported that 81 percent of the teenage fathers in their sample still dated the mother during pregnancy and after childbirth; 75.6 percent helped her by giving her money and 85.3 percent helped her in other ways such as transportation and gifts while she was pregnant. After the baby was born, these figures rose to 83 percent, 88 percent, and 92 percent, respectively. Other reports (Barret & Robinson 1982, Connolly 1978, Hendricks 1980, Howard 1975, Johnson 1978, Pannor & Evans 1975) noted that adolescent fathers are interested in the mother and baby and that they are eager to talk and become involved in the fathering experience.

Over the past five years the Reverend Richard Banks, Curate of Christ The King Center in Charlotte, North Carolina, has noticed a marked change in the behaviors of low-income black teen fathers:

> They no longer abandon their children. They are more responsible than that. Even though there are fewer marriages, I see a lot more involvement as fathers work to support their child. Although the mother is the main breadwinner, the father provides the extras even in those cases where relationships with the mother have gone by the wayside. It is rare today to find a child of teenage parents who does not know his daddy. Part of this involvement is due to black men being aware of their role as nurturer and provider, rather than just procreator.

Conclusion

In light of the absence of scientific information on teenage fathers, the professional community has relied on stereotypes from the 1940s into the 1980s. Although some young fathers may fit this stereotype, most do not. A growing body of research has dispelled five commonly cited myths about adolescent fathers that were borne out of the sociological context in which laws were made and research conducted. It is obvious from the profile presented in this chapter that teenage fathers need support and guidance rather than downgrading, a purpose past stereotypes have traditionally served. Causes of teenage pregnancy that have been documented by research are developmental explanations, lack of sex education, and a generational cycle that occurs through poverty, attitudes, and role modeling. Despite the overabundance of myths, teen fathers must face hard truths and tragic consequences. In the next chapter I will discuss the consequences of teenage fatherhood that lead to economic and educational hardships, relationship problems, as well as parenting limitations for young fathers and mothers.

References

Alan Guttmacher Institute. (1982) *Teenage pregnancy: The problem that hasn't gone away.* New York: Alan Guttmacher Institute.

Allen-Meares, P. (1984) Adolescent pregnancy and parenting: The forgotten adolescent father and his parents. *Journal of Social Work & Human Sexuality* 3:27–38.

Baldwin, W., & Cain, V.S. (1980) The children of teenage parents. *Family Planning Perspectives* 12:34–43.

Barret, R.L., & Robinson, B.E. (1982) A descriptive study of teenage expectant fathers. *Family Relations* 31:349–52.

———. (1987) "The role of adolescent fathers in parenting and childrearing." In A.R. Stiffman & R.A. Feldman (eds.), *Advances in adolescent mental health. Vol. IV, Childbearing and childrearing.* Greenwich, Conn.: JAI Press.

Brown, S.V. (1983) The commitment and concerns of black adolescent parents. *Social Work Research & Abstracts* 19:27–34.

Caparulo, F., & London, K. (1981) Adolescent fathers: Adolescents first, fathers second. *Issues in Health Care of Women* 3:23–33.

Card, J.J. (1981) Long-term consequences for children of teenage parents. *Demography* 18:137–56.

Card, J.J., & Wise, L.L. (1978) Teenage mothers and teenage fathers: The impact of early childbearing on the parents' personal and professional lives. *Family Planning Perspectives* 10:199–205.

Children's Defense Fund. (1986) The broader challenge of teen pregnancy prevention. *Children's Defense Fund Reports* 8:1, 6, and 8.

Connolly, L. (1978) Boy fathers. *Human Behavior*:40–43.

de Lissovoy, V. (1973a) Child care by adolescent parents. *Children Today* 2:22–25.
———. (1973b) High school marriages: A longitudinal study. *Journal of Marriage and the Family* 35:245–55.
Earls, F., & Siegel, B. (1980) Precocious fathers. *American Journal of Orthopsychiatry* 50:469–80.
Elster, A.B., & Lamb, M. (1982) Adolescent fathers: A group potentially at risk for parenting failure. *Infant Mental Health Journal* 3:148–55.
Elster, A.B., & Panzarine, S. (1980) Unwed teenage fathers: Emotional and health educational needs. *Journal of Adolescent Health Care* 1:116–20.
———. (1983a) "Adolescent fathers." In E.R. McAnarney (ed.), *Premature adolescent pregnancy and parenthood,* pp. 231–52. New York: Grune & Stratton.
———. (1983b) Teenage fathers: Stresses during gestation and early parenthood. *Clinical Pediatrics* 22:700–703.
Field, T., Widmayer, S.M., Stringer, S., & Ignatoff, E. (1980) Teenage, lower-class black mothers and their preterm infants: An intervention and developmental follow-up. *Child Development* 51:426–36.
Finkel, M., & Finkel, D. (1975) Sexual and contraceptive knowledge, attitudes, and behavior of male adolescents. *Family Planning Perspectives* 7:256–60.
Fry, P.S., & Trifiletti, R.J. (1983) Teenage fathers: An exploration of their developmental needs and anxieties and the implications for clinical-social intervention services. *Journal of Psychiatric Treatment and Evaluation* 5:219–27.
Furstenberg, F.F. (1976) *Unplanned parenthood: The social consequences of teenage childbearing.* New York: The Free Press.
Futterman, S., & Livermore, J.B. (1947) Putative fathers. *Journal of Social Casework* 28:174–78.
Gabbard, G.O., & Wolff, J.R. (1977) The unwed pregnant teenager and her male relationship. *The Journal of Reproductive Medicine* 19:137–40.
Group for the Advancement of Psychiatry. (1986) *Teenage pregnancy: Impact on adolescent development.* New York: Brunner/Mazel.
Harrison, C.E. (1982) "Teenage pregnancy." In D.L. Parron & L. Eisenberg (eds.), *Infants at risk for developmental dysfunction,* pp. 43–55. Washington, D.C.: National Academy Press.
Hendricks, L.W. (1980) Unwed adolescent fathers: Problems they face and their sources of social support. *Adolescence* 15:861–69.
———. (1982) Unmarried black adolescent fathers' attitudes toward abortion, contraception, and sexuality: A preliminary report. *Journal of Adolescent Health Care* 2:199–203.
———. (1983) Suggestions for reaching unmarried black adolescent fathers. *Child Welfare* 62:141–46.
Hendriks, L.E., Howard, C.S., & Caesar, P.O. (1981) Help-seeking behavior among select populations of black unmarried adolescent fathers: Implications for human service agencies. *American Journal of Public Health* 71:733–35.
Hobson, C.F., Robinson, B.E., & Skeen, P. (1983) *Child development and relationships.* New York: Random House.
Howard, M. (1975). "Improving services for young fathers." In *Sharing.* Washington, D.C.: Child Welfare League of America.

Inselberg, R.M. (1962) Marital problems and satisfaction in high school marriages. *Marriage and Family Living* 24:74–77.

Johnson, L.B., & Staples, R.E. (1979) Family planning and the young minority male: A pilot project. *The Family Coordinator* 28:535–43.

Johnson, S. (15 March 1978) Two pioneer programs help unwed teenage fathers cope. *The New York Times,* 54.

Kasanin, J., & Handschin, S. (1941) Psychodynamic factors in illegitimacy. *American Journal of Orthopsychiatry* 11:66–84.

Kerckhoff, A.C., & Parrow, A.A. (1979) The effect of early marriage and the educational attainment of young men. *Journal of Marriage and the Family* 41:97–107.

Kinard, E.M., & Klerman, L.V. (1980) Teenage parenting and child abuse: Are they related? *American Journal of Orthopsychiatry* 59:481–88.

Klerman, L. (1982) "Teenage parents: A brief review of research." In D.L. Parron & L. Eisenberg (eds.), *Infants at risk for developmental dysfunction,* pp. 125–32. Washington, D.C.: National Academy Press.

Klerman, L.V., & Jekel, J.F. (1973) *School-age mothers: Problems, programs, and policy.* Hamden, Conn.: Shoe String Press.

Lamb, M.E., & Elster, A.B. (1985). Adolescent mother-father relationships. *Developmental Psychology* 21:768–73.

Leashore, B.R. (1979). Human services and the unmarried father: The forgotten half. *The Family Coordinator* 28:529–34.

Leppert, P.C. (1984) The effect of pregnancy on adolescent growth and development. *Women and Health* 9:2–3, 65–79.

Lorenzi, M.E., Klerman, L.V., & Jekel, J.F. (1977) School-age parents: How permanent a relationship? *Adolescence* 12:13–22.

McCoy, J.E., & Tyler, F.B. (1985) Selected psychosocial characteristics of black unwed adolescent fathers. *Journal of Adolescent Health Care* 6:12–16.

Moore, K.A., & Burt, M.R. (1982) *Private crisis, public cost: Policy perspectives on teenage childbearing.* Washington, D.C.: The Urban Institute.

Nakashima, I.I., & Camp, B.W. (1984) Fathers of infants born to adolescent mothers. *American Journal of Diseases of Children* 138:452–54.

National Center for Health Statistics. (1981) Advance report of final natality statistics, 1979. *Monthly Vital Statistics Report* (DHHS Publication No. PHS 81-1120). Hyattsville, Maryland: Public Health Services.

———. (1984) Advance report of final natality statistics, 1982. *Monthly Vital Statistics Report* (DDHS Publication No. PHS 84-1120). Hyattsville, Maryland: Public Health Services.

Nettleton, C.A., & Cline, D.W. (1975) Dating patterns, sexual relationships and use of contraceptives of 700 unwed mothers during a two-year period following delivery. *Adolescence* 37:45–57.

Nye, F.I., & Lamberts, M.B. (1980) *School-age parenthood: Consequences for babies, mothers, fathers, grandparents, and others.* Washington State University Cooperative Extension Bulletin 0667. Pullman, Washington; Washington State University.

Pannor, R., & Evans, B.W. (1965) The unmarried father: An integral part of casework services to the unmarried mother. *Child Welfare* 44:15–20.

———. (1975) The unmarried father revisited. *The Journal of School Health* 45:286–91.

Pannor, R., Massarik, F., & Evans, B. (1971) *The unmarried father: New approaches for helping unmarried young parents.* New York: Springer.

Panzarine, S., & Elster, A.B. (1983) Coping in a group of expectant adolescent fathers: An exploratory study. *Journal of Adolescent Health Care* 4:117–20.

Pauker, J.D. (1971) Fathers of children conceived out of wedlock: Pregnancy, high school, psychological test results. *Developmental Psychology* 4:215–18.

Phipps-Yonas, S. (1980) Teenage pregnancy and motherhood: A review of the literature. *American Journal of Orthopsychiatry* 59:403–31.

Platts, H.K. (1968) A public adoption agency's approach to natural fathers. *Child Welfare* 47:530–37.

Price, L. (1954) *Out of wedlock.* New York: McGraw-Hill.

Redmond, M.A. (1985) Attitudes of adolescent males toward adolescent pregnancy and fatherhood. *Family Relations* 34:337–42.

Reider, N. (1948) The unmarried father. *American Journal of Orthopsychiatry* 18:230–37.

Rivara, F.P. (1981) Teenage pregnancy: The forgotten father. *Developmental Behavioral Pediatrics* 2:141–46.

Rivara, F.P., Sweeney, P.J., & Henderson, B.F. (1985) A study of low socioeconomic status, black teenage fathers and their nonfather peers. *Pediatrics* 75:648–56.

———. (1986) Black teenage fathers: What happens when the child is born? *Pediatrics* 78:151–58.

Robbins, M.B., & Lynn, D.B. (1973) The unwed fathers: Generation recidivism and attitudes about intercourse in California Youth Authority wards. *Journal of Sex Research* 9:334–41.

Robinson, B.E., & Barret, R.L. (1985, December). Teenage fathers. *Psychology Today* 19:66–70.

———. (1986) *The developing father: Emerging roles in contemporary society.* New York: Guilford.

———. (1987, May 27). Myths about adolescent fathers with policy change implications for health care professionals. Paper presented at the Association for the Care of Children's Health 22nd Annual Conference, Halifax, Nova Scotia.

Robinson, B.E., Barret, R.L., & Skeen, P. (1983) Locus of control of unwed adolescent fathers versus adolescent nonfathers. *Perceptual and Motor Skills* 56:397–98.

Roosa, M.W., Fitzgerald, H.E., & Carlson, N.A. A comparison of teenage and older mothers: A systems analysis. *Journal of Marriage and the Family* 44:367–77.

Ross, A. (1982) *Teenage mothers, teenage fathers.* New York: Everest House.

Rothstein, A.A. (1978) Adolescent males, fatherhood, and abortion. *Journal of Youth and Adolescence* 7:203–14.

Rus-Eft, D., Sprenger, M., & Beever, H. (1979) Antecedents of adolescent parenthood and consequences at age 30. *The Family Coordinator* 28:173–79.

Scales, P., & Gordon, S. (1979) Preparing today's youth for tomorrow's family. *Journal of the Institute for Family Research and Education* 1:3–7.

Silk, S.D. (1981, August) Cognitive and social correlates of adolescent pregnancy.

Paper presented at the American Psychological Association, Los Angeles, California.

Simkins, L. (1984) Consequences of teenage pregnancy and motherhood. *Adolescence* 19:39–54.

Sonenstein, F.L. (1986) "Risking paternity: Sex and contraception among adolescent males." In A.B. Elster & M. Lamb (eds.), pp. 31–54. *Adolescent fatherhood.* Hillsdale, New Jersey: Lawrence Erlbaum.

Stengel, R. (9 December 1985) The missing father myth. *Time*:90.

Unger, D.G., & Wandersman, L.P. (1985) Social support and adolescent mothers: Action research contributions to theory and application. *Journal of Social Issues* 41:29–45.

Vaz, R., Smolen, P., & Miller, C. (1983) Adolescent pregnancy: Involvement of the male partner. *Journal of Adolescent Health Care* 4:246–50.

Vincent, C.E. (1956) *Unwed mothers.* New York: The Free Press.

———. (1960) Unmarried fathers and the mores: "Sexual exploiter" as an ex post facto label. *American Sociological Review* 25:40–46.

Welcher, D.W. (1982) "The effect of early childbearing on the psychosocial development of adolescent parents." In D.L. Parron & L. Eisenberg (ed.), pp. 115–23. *Infants at risk for developmental dysfunction.* Washington, D.C.: National Academy Press.

Westney, O.E., Cole, O.J., & Munford, T.L. (1986) Adolescent unwed prospective fathers: Readiness for fatherhood and behaviors toward the mother and the expected infant. *Adolescence* 21:901–11.

Wulf, D. (1985) Doing something about teenage pregnancy. *Family Planning Perspective* 17:52.

Young, L. (1954) *Out of Wedlock,* New York: McGraw-Hill.

Zabin, L.S., Hirsch, M.B., Smith, E.A., Streett, R., & Hardy, J.B. (1986) Evaluation of a pregnancy prevention program for urban teenagers. *Family Planning Perspectives* 18:119–26.

Zelnik, M., Kantner, J.F., & Ford, K. (1981) *Sex and pregnancy in adolescence.* Beverly Hills, Ca.: Sage.

3
Hard Truths and Tragic Consequences

> Pregnancy among unmarried teens is a problem for both the girls hav-
> ing babies and the boys who father them. And it is a problem we all
> must face . . . not just the government, but all of us.
> —Health and Human Services Secretary, Otis R. Bowen (1986)

*Many of the teenage fathers I talked with felt unprepared for the conse-
quences that parenthood brought. Seventeen-year-old Walton is a case in
point:*

*"Boy, I sure was surprised about my baby. I'd never been around babies
much before, and for the longest time I just knew something was wrong with
her. She didn't make much noise unless she was crying, and she slept all the
time. I'm telling you, it was a real drag!"*

*Walton and his 17-year-old girlfriend Algia are still in high school and
depend on their parents to help with finances and taking care of their newborn baby. Money is tight and the grandparents pitch in whenever and wher-
ever they can. Walton works in a mill and Algia babysits for a neighbor.*

*Walton is always wanting to spend money on his motorcycle, but he
remembers that there are bills to pay and diapers, food, and clothes to buy.
Both Walton and Algia confess that there are times when they forget that
they have a baby. Walton plays basketball in high school and Algia and her
baby just pack up and go to the ballgames when he plays. But when they
went to the prom, grandparents were more than willing to babysit.*

Walton is only one illustration of how unfamiliar and uncomfortable teenage
males feel with the responsibilities of parenthood. This discomfort, coupled
with educational and economic hurdles, propels young fathers and mothers
into a lifelong, never-ending cycle of socioeconomic misery, broken relationships, and parenting frustration.

The consequences of parenthood for adolescent males can be devastating
in a number of ways. The typical teenage father is single at the conception
of his child, has little education, unsteady employment, and a salary only
slightly above minimum wage. His child is more likely to be born premature
or to have an obstetrical problem at birth. The father and mother, still children themselves, have unrealistic ideas of marriage and children and their

baby is at higher than average risk for abuse. If the father and mother marry, their chances for making the marriage work are slim. The child is likely to be raised in poverty and to someday become an adolescent parent as well—thus the cycle is perpetuated. In this chapter I will discuss what research has revealed about these consequences in terms of education and economic status, durability of the father-mother relationship, and outcomes for the children of adolescent parents.

Educational and Economic Consequences

Pregnancy or parenthood often is the final factor prompting many young men and women who already were lagging behind in school to drop out (Children's Defense Fund 1986). Research has consistently shown that unplanned and premature parenthood preempts the educational, vocational, and social experiences of the adolescent that are essential to prepare him for his adult roles (Allen-Meares 1984). Studies also have revealed that vocational-educational concerns are the number one stressor that teenage fathers say they must face (Elster & Panzarine 1983b).

Using data from Project Talent, a nationwide study to identify the characteristics of talented adolescents, Josefina Card and Lauress Wise (1978) analyzed responses of a nationwide random sample consisting of 375,000 boys and girls from 1,225 senior and junior high schools. The survey polled the subjects one year, five years, and eleven years after they completed high school. Teenage parents were defined as those who became parents before their twentieth birthday. A contrasting sample was made up of some of their classmates who were not parents as of their twentieth birthday.

Both adolescent fathers and mothers obtained substantially less education than their classmates. The younger they were at the time of their child's birth, the more severe the educational setback they endured. The boys and girls who became teenage parents reported having lower income levels and lower academic abilities at age 15 than their classmates. They also had lower educational aspirations. As a result of their investigation, Card and Wise concluded that, regardless of background factors, teenage parenthood is a direct cause of "truncated" schooling, a factor that causes teenage fathers to occupy lower prestige blue collar jobs and to enter the labor force earlier than their unmarried classmates.

Card and Wise also found that young fathers were more likely than young mothers to be single at the conception and birth of their child. The proportion of teenage fathers and mothers who were separated or divorced was higher than that of their classmates at each follow-up period. At five and eleven years after high school, teenage fathers and mothers had been married more times than their classmates. Because teenage childbearers have longer reproductive careers, adolescent fathers and mothers had more children than their classmates at the five and eleven year follow-up periods.

Also drawing from the Project Talent data pool, Darlene Rus-Eft, Marlene Sprenger, and Anne Beever (1979) studied the antecedents and consequences of early childbearing by in-depth interviews of 500 men and 500 women who had participated in Project Talent as teenagers. They found unfinished schooling, low-level employment, low-paying positions, higher numbers of children than average, and higher than average rates of divorce to be linked to adolescent fatherhood and motherhood.

Kerckhoff and Parrow (1979) studied the effect of early marriage on the educational attainment of young men. Using data from the National Longitudinal Surveys of Labor Market Experience, the researchers examined data on 5,225 unmarried males between the ages of 15 and 18 from 1966 to 1970. Findings indicated that early marriage in high school delayed educational attainment for both black and white males. Not only had these young married men made less educational progress during a four-year period, they were also less likely than an unmarried comparison group to be in school four years later and they had lower educational goals later on as well.

A more recent longitudinal study (Rivara, Sweeney & Henderson 1986) followed the lives of eighty-one teen fathers from the time of their girlfriend's pregnancy to nine and eighteen months postpartum and compared them to nonfather adolescents. After eighteen months, more fathers were heads of households and more of them had dropped out of school. The majority of the fathers, although unmarried, lived with the mother or had daily or weekly contact with her and the baby.

Overall these studies indicate that inadequate education and poor work skills lead to low-paying jobs, poverty, and ultimately welfare. In New York City, 72 percent of 15-to 17-year-old mothers who gave birth were supported by Aid to Families of Dependent Children (Simkins 1984). And welfare dependence increases as the age of the mother decreases. One-third of the mothers who had their first child between the ages of 13 and 15 lived below the federal poverty level—2.6 times greater than those who bore children after 20 years of age (Simkins 1984).

Consequences of the Father-Mother Relationship

As discussed in chapter 2, the relationships between adolescent fathers and mothers are not fleeting affairs. Research indicates, however, that over a long-term basis these relationships do not flourish either. The obstacles that young parents are up against make it difficult for relationships to last.

Short-Term Follow-up

A number of studies reported the teen father's relationship with the mother over various periods of time after childbirth. Although pregnant teenagers marry only about 10 percent of the time, an impressive number of young fathers in these studies maintained relationships. At twelve months after childbirth, half of the unwed adolescent parents continued to date each other (Nettleton & Cline 1975). At fifteen months after the baby's birth, 64 percent of the teenage fathers in another study continued to contribute financially to the support of the mother and baby (Lorenzi, Klerman & Jekel 1977). After eighteen months postpartum, most of the eighty-one teenage fathers in another investigation continued to be involved in the lives of the mother and child (Rivara, Sweeney & Henderson 1986). Overall, 34 percent of the fathers had decreased their contact with the mothers, 19 percent increased their contact, and 47 percent said there was no change in contact during the eighteen-month time period. Only three fathers had no contact with their children; 11 percent lived with the child, and another 25 percent to 36 percent saw the child daily. Only 12 percent of the infants lived with both parents. Fully 95 percent of the fathers said that they were contributing financially to the care of their child, although this amounted to less than twenty-five dollars per week. A total of 53 percent of the children carried their father's last name, and 68 percent of male children had their father's first name.

The Bank Street College of Education coordinated a program in eight cities that offered vocational assistance, counseling, and classes in prenatal development and parenting. Four hundred teenage fathers participated. At the end of two years, 82 percent had daily contact with their children, 74 percent provided financial support, and 90 percent still had relationships with the mothers of their babies (Stengel 1985).

Teenage Marriages

Adolescent marriages tend to have greater discord (de Lissovoy 1973b, Nakashima & Camp 1984) and higher divorce rates (Inselberg 1962, McCarthy & Menken 1979) than adult marriages. The divorce rate for parents younger than 18 is three times greater than that for parents who have their first child after age 20, and it is greater for couples with premarital pregnancies than for those who conceive after marriage (Furstenberg 1976, Nye & Lamberts 1980). Much of the marital stress comes from parenting and financial demands, as 19-year-old teen father Henry shared with me:

> My wife and I just don't get enough time together anymore. We can't do
> some of the things we'd like to do like just run out and see a movie. We

always have to worry about a baby sitter—a sister sitter—or whatever you want to call her. And you know, it just puts a strain on our marriage 'cause we don't get time to talk much more. If we get in bed and try to talk, the baby will be crying in the next five minutes. They're just always there and you can't run from them.

A longitudinal follow-up study of thirty-seven couples over a three-year period indicated that, although after thirty months 77 percent of the teenage couples stayed together, marital tensions were evident (de Lissovoy 1973b). Young moms and dads had grown more dissatisfied with their marriages, especially in regard to childrearing and family income. Other data suggest that 44 percent of young women who give birth between the ages of 14 and 17 are divorced fifteen years later (Alan Guttmacher Institute 1982). Some experts suggest that unrealistic expectations of the marital relationship may contribute to the demise of marriages among adolescent couples (Nakashima & Camp 1984).

Long-Term Follow-up

The longest longitudinal study was conducted by Frank Furstenberg (1976), who followed adolescent mothers under age 18 for five years. The teenagers were interviewed when they registered at the prenatal clinic at Baltimore's Sinai Hospital between 1966 and 1968. They were interviewed at three additional times: one year after childbirth, again in 1970, and last in 1972, when their child was five years old. Interviews were also conducted with as many fathers as could be found. Of the 33 percent located, over half were residing with the young mothers in the study during the period of the interviews.

Few marriages that occurred among the adolescents lasted through the five-year study. Still, it was among the few stable marriages in the group that father-child contact was most intense and father-child relationships the most satisfying. Children of parents who never married were as likely to see their fathers regularly as those whose parents had previously been married. Approximately 25 percent of the fathers visited their child at least once a week, and one-third gave economic support, regardless of whether they had been married to the mother. In general single fathers tended to be emotionally closer to their children than previously married fathers were. Approximately 63 percent of all the fathers maintained contact with their children five years after childbirth, and 30 percent who lived outside the mother's home maintained cordial relationships and visited regularly.

Furstenberg discovered from follow-up interviews with the original sample that children of parents who did not marry were frequently named after the father (Furstenberg & Talvitie 1980). He and his associates described this practice as a deliberate attempt by both parents to strengthen the father-child bond, with the name serving as a reminder of the biological tie. Just over 20 percent of the young women involved their partners in selecting their child's name; most of this group planned to marry. At birth approximately 50 percent of the male babies received their father's first name, middle name, or both. In addition, 43 percent of the girls born were given their father's last name, even when their parents remained unmarried. There was a consistent association between naming patterns and father-child contact. Children receiving their father's name, for instance, were more likely to have regular contact with their father and to receive economic assistance from him. Furstenberg and Talvitie (1980) suggest that "the bestowal of the father's name may be nothing more than an expression of prior sentiment, an acknowledgement of the father's willingness at the time of birth to play an active part in the child's upbringing" (p. 49).

Consequences for Children of Teenage Parents

Children of teenage parents run the triple risk of being unwanted, born into poverty, and exposed to inadequate parenting. Also there is a good chance that they will develop later behavioral and emotional problems (Harrison 1982).

Developmental Outcomes

Prenatal complications such as toxemia, preeclampsia, and prolonged labor are more common among teenage mothers than adult mothers (Simkins 1984). Also, compared to the offspring of adult parents, newborns of teenage parents are more likely to suffer from prematurity, birth defects, mental retardation, and other health problems that often result in death during the first year (Field et al. 1980, Nye & Lamberts 1980, Simkins 1984). These health problems occur partly because young mothers have not reached their full biological maturity and because they have poor diets and inadequate prenatal care. Adolescents are twice as likely as adult mothers to miss prenatal care during the first six months of their pregnancies (Scales & Gordon 1979). Recent statistics indicate that only 49 percent of women age 15 to 17 who gave birth in 1981 and 59 percent of those age 18 to 19 obtained prenatal care in the first trimester of pregnancy, compared with 76 percent of pregnant women of all ages (Wulf 1986).

Long-Term Consequences

Research suggests that at 6 years of age, children of teenage parents—compared to children of adult parents—have lower intelligence test scores, are more dependent and distractable, are labeled by teachers as behavior problems, and are behind in reading ability (Roosa, Fitzgerald & Carlson 1982). At 4 years of age, children of teenage parents tend to be overly conforming and noncommunicative, and at 7 they are more hostile, resentful of authority, and likely to suffer from speech difficulties as well as school maladjustment (Maracek 1979).

Longitudinal data from the Johns Hopkins Child Development Study demonstrated that at 8 months, 4 years, 7 years, and 12 years of age, children of adolescent parents had more emotional and behavioral problems and lower achievement than children born to older mothers (Welcher 1982). Additional long-term data even revealed differences between children of adolescent and older parents when the offspring grew up and attended high school (Card 1981). During their teenage years, children of adolescent parents had lower scores on intelligence tests and lower educational expectations than their classmates. Children of teenagers also were less sociable, less tidy, less cultured, and less mature than their peers. An 11-year follow-up showed that, when compared to their classmates, children of teenage parents actually had completed less education, had married at an earlier age, and had married more times. Thus, children of adolescents tended to repeat the early marriage, early parenthood, and higher fertility cycle of their parents.

At one time it was believed that the young age of the parents caused these developmental problems in the offspring. However, several reports from numerous different research studies have shown no significant differences between children born to teenagers and those born to older mothers and fathers on the same factors as discussed previously (Kinard & Reinherz 1984, Simkins 1984). These conflicting findings have led experts to conclude that other factors are correlated with parental age—mainly socioeconomic status—and are responsible for the negative outcomes among children born to adolescent parents (Baldwin & Cain 1980; Klerman 1982; Lamb & Elster 1985; Roosa, Fitzgerald & Carlson 1982). Quality of prenatal and postnatal care and whether there are other caretakers in addition to the adolescent mother are additional correlates (Simkins 1984). In their comparison study of teenage and adult mothers and their offspring Roosa, Fitzgerald, and Carlson (1982) found that in every case, the influence of socioeconomic status was several times the size of the influence of age. Klerman (1982) also suggests that poverty and its associated lifestyle are conditions to which infants are particularly vulnerable and that parents are not randomly distributed throughout the teenage population. On the contrary, they are concentrated within low-income families where early sexual activity, inadequate contraception use, and reluctance to seek abortions are all found more frequently.

Inadequate Parenting

Inadequate parenting is an additional risk for children of adolescent parents. Both fathers and mothers have unrealistic childrearing attitudes and a misunderstanding of children's developmental milestones—such as when they should begin walking, talking, or become toilet trained (de Lissovoy 1973a; Field et al. 1980; Rivara, Sweeney & Henderson 1986).

A longitudinal study by Rivara, Sweeney, and Henderson (1986) indicated that eighteen months after childbirth, fewer adolescent fathers, compared to a group of nonfathers, knew the normal development and normal diet of a newborn—although all teenagers had limited knowledge. Only 42 percent of the fathers knew what a normal body temperature was and one-fourth from each group believed that watching television would increase the creative imagination of children. Lack of such information can cause parents to place undue pressure on their children to perform certain developmental tasks before they are ready.

De Lissovoy (1973a), for example, interviewed forty-eight adolescent married fathers and mothers and found them to be emotionally and intellectually unprepared for parenthood. They had unrealistic expectations of their children and showed impatience and intolerance which frequently resulted in physical means of disciplining children. The author concluded that the young parents were undergoing severe frustrations, and that their unrealistic expectations of child development, the general disappointment in their lives, and their lack of economic resources served to raise their irritability and lower their threshold of tolerance.

During one visit to a young father, the author observed him spank his 7-month-old baby who had pulled the nipple from his bottle and spilled the contents in his crib:

> Although I pointed out that the bottle was probably spilled because the nipple was not put in correctly, the father said, "He has been asking for this all day." Obviously, coping with the baby's daily demands was a difficult task for this young father. (de Lissovoy 1973a, p. 25)

Thus, it is not surprising that infants of adolescent parents are at higher risk for child abuse than offspring of older parents (Kinard & Klerman 1980). Data indicate, in fact, that the younger the parent, the greater the risk for child abuse (Oates et al. 1979). As a rule, adolescent parents do not possess the emotional and maturational skills necessary for adequate parenting. Risk factors associated with parents who are more likely to abuse their children perfectly match the profile of adolescent parents: unplanned births, infants with birth defects or obstetrical problems, and having children to satisfy unmet emotional needs (Simkins 1984, Zuravin 1987).

The degree to which lack of child development information might influence father-child interactions is another factor that is not fully understood. In a recent study teenage fathers and older fathers were observed interacting with their infants (Lamb & Elster 1985). Fathers were rated vis-à-vis their infants on responsiveness, stimulation and arousal, caregiving, displays of positive affection, and reading/watching television. Overall teenage fathers behaved no differently with their babies than older fathers. The researchers concluded that age of father does not appear to have a significant impact on the early social experiences of infants with adolescent parents. Still, the combination of factors that induce stress in adolescent fathers during pregnancy and parenthood puts these young men at risk for parenting failure (Elster & Lamb 1982). Prolonged educational deficiencies, dissatisfaction with their jobs, feelings of being economically strapped, inadequate knowledge of children and childrearing, and potential relationship conflicts (or marital instability) are all factors that diminish the quality of adolescent fathering capacity.

Fathering Influences

An entire body of research has shown that fathers have positive effects on their children's social and cognitive development (Robinson & Barret 1986). The father's absence also can have a negative impact on children. Although research on teenage fathers is very scanty in this area, there appears to be a link between the continuity of the young father's relationship with his child and his offspring's social and cognitive development.

Frank Furstenberg (1976) found from studying teenage fathers that when they actively participate in their children's development, their children are less likely to have behavioral problems. In contrast, when adolescent fathers were absent from the home, children were more likely to have behavioral problems, lower self-esteem, lower trust levels, and poor social competence in general. In homes where teenage fathers and mothers married early and where the marriage endured, the cognitive abilities of their children were superior, compared to children from households where fathers visited only occasionally or maintained no contact at all.

Research also indicates that the young mother's social network, including how she perceives the teenage father's support, can have a positive or negative bearing on the child (Unger & Wandersman 1985). When adolescent mothers felt they had social support and received child care assistance from the baby's father, the infants were more responsive. Thus teenage fathers even influence their children's welfare in indirect ways. It has been suggested further that the circumstances surrounding adolescent fatherhood may combine to make teenage males inadequate sources of social support for their partners which, in turn, may have adverse, indirect effects on the children's development (Elster & Lamb 1982). Overly stressed himself, the young father may be depleted in the required energy to invest emotionally or respond sensitively to the infant's signals and needs. Although unsubstantiated by research, Frank Bolton and Jay Belsky (1986) suspect that adolescent fathers suffer from greater pressures than adolescent mothers:

The fathers may be more personally violent, have difficulty with drug and alcohol abuse, and/or have greater difficulty in controlling their temper. In an indirect fashion, they may have had their plans more severely curtailed by the births, may feel themselves to be more isolated from their children and support systems, and may be shackled by an overwhelming helplessness in seeking to contribute to their children's lives. (p. 136)

Breaking the Cycle

Most measures aimed at reducing adolescent pregnancy are remedial in nature. Such programs are needed to encourage teen fathers to stay in school and finish their formal education so that they do not end up unskilled and unemployed. Other remedial programs are needed to give those fathers who want to participate fully in the childbirth experience classes in prenatal development, nutrition, and prepared childbirth. In this way they can receive optimum benefit from the experience. Other intervention programs need to inform young fathers about normal infant and child development and to provide guidance in the proper guidance and discipline of their child.

Although important, remedial programs are only temporary solutions. They are band-aids over festering wounds. The cycle of teenage pregnancy can only be broken through preventive programs that begin not in adolescence, but when children begin preschool. Sex education and family life education, taught in a developmentally appropriate way at each age, must be compulsory from the preschool to high school. We already have tentative evidence that preschool education can have long-reaching effects twenty years later and may be a factor in helping break the cycle of poverty as well as the cycle of teenage pregnancy (Clement et al. 1984). The longitudinal research of David Weikart and his colleagues at the High Scope Project in Ypsilanti, Michigan, followed children in a high-quality preschool program (The Perry Preschool Project) through the end of adolescence. Measures studied included pregnancy rates, social behaviors in the community at large, job training, college attendance, and patterns of crime. The results were staggering. Preschool education appeared to reduce the rate of teenage pregnancies. The Perry Preschool Project reported a 64 per 100 pregnancy and live-birth rate for teenagers who went to preschool, as opposed to a 117 per 100 rate for those who did not attend preschool. Even more dramatic was the finding that after pregnancy and childbirth, 88 percent of the adolescent mothers who had attended preschool were more likely to return and complete high school, compared with only 30 percent of mothers who had not gone to preschool.

The High Scope study is the first to show that early childhood education can help prevent adolescent pregnancy and delinquency, as well as improve the likelihood of school completion, employment after high school completion, reduced dependence on welfare, and long-term socioeconomic improvement in a disadvantaged population. These findings have strong policy implications for educational reform and suggest that there is something that can be done with children prior to school (namely preschool education) that will help them traverse the formal educational system more efficiently, with higher attainment, and with direct effects on early socioeconomic success.

Conclusion

Teenage fathers face overwhelming odds against success in parenting, child-rearing, and marital relationships. The long-term solutions lie in an early education in which a solid foundation of knowledge and responsibility is laid from the preschool years. More immediate solutions, however, are needed to help young men who are already fathers to become more competent ones. Current evidence shows that of those who complete a program, the majority turn out to be responsible and caring parents (Stengel 1985).

Teenage fathers need counseling to help them deal with the stresses surrounding the anticipated childbirth and how to reconcile the competing role requirements of the teenage years and parenthood. They need vocational counseling so that their good intentions of providing financial support can be realized through education and occupational planning. They need counseling to deal with the stresses of financial responsibilities and problems in their marriages or their relationships with the mother of their child. I will discuss more fully these needs and how they can be addressed by the helping professions in chapter 5 and by program development in chapter 6. Meanwhile, in the next chapter, I will explore the psychological adjustment of teenage fathers, as it compares to teenage nonfathers and adult men.

References

Alan Guttmacher Institute. (1982) *Teenage pregnancy: The problem that hasn't gone away*. New York: Alan Guttmacher Institute.

Allen-Meares, P. (1984) Adolescent pregnancy and parenting: The forgotten adolescent father and his parents. *Journal of Social Work & Human Sexuality* 3:27–38.

Baldwin, W., & Cain, V.S. (1980) The children of teenage parents. *Family Planning Perspectives* 12:34–43.

Bolton, F.G. (1980). *The pregnant adolescent: Problems of premature parenthood*. Beverly Hills, Ca.: Sage.

Bolton, F.G., & Belsky, J. (1986) "The adolescent father and child maltreatment."

In A.B. Elster & M.E. Lamb (eds.), *Adolescent fatherhood,* pp. 123–40. Hillsdale, New Jersey: Lawrence Erlbaum.

Card, J.J. (1981) Long-term consequences for children of teenage parents. *Demography* 18:137–56.

Card, J.J., & Wise, L.L. (1978) Teenage mothers and teenage fathers: The impact of early childbearing on the parents' personal and professional lives. *Family Planning Perspectives* 10:199–205.

Children's Defense Fund. (1986) The broader challenge of teen pregnancy prevention. *Children's Defense Fund Reports* 8:1, 6, and 8.

Clement, J.R., Schweinhart, L.J., Barnett, W.S., Epstein, A.S., & Weikart, D.P. (1984) *Changed lives: The effects of the Perry Preschool Program on youths through age 19.* Ypsilanti, Michigan: The High Scope Press.

de Lissovoy, V. (1973a) Child care by adolescent parents. *Children Today* 2:22–25.

———. (1973b) High school marriages: A longitudinal study. *Journal of Marriage and the Family* 35:245–55.

Elster, A.B., & Lamb, M.E. (1982) Adolescent fathers: A group potentially at risk for parenting failure. *Infant Mental Health Journal* 3:148–55.

Elster, A.B., & Panzarine, S. (1983a) Adolescent fathers. In E.R. McAnarney (ed.), *Premature adolescent pregnancy and parenthood.* pp. 231–52. New York: Grune & Stratton.

———. (1983b) Teenage fathers: Stresses during gestation and early parenthood. *Clinical Pediatrics* 22:700–703.

Field, T., Widmayer, S.M., Stringer, S., & Ignatoff, E. (1980) Teenage, lower-class black mothers and their preterm infants: An intervention and developmental follow-up. *Child Development* 51:426–36.

Furstenberg, F.F. (1976) *Unplanned parenthood: The social consequences of teenage childbearing.* New York: The Free Press.

Furstenberg, F.F., & Talvitie, K.G. (1980) Children's names and paternal claims: Bonds between unmarried fathers and their children. *Journal of Family Issues* 1:31–57.

Harrison, C.E. (1982) "Teenage pregnancy." In D.L. Parron & L. Eisenberg (eds.), pp. 43–55. *Infants at risk for developmental dysfunction.* Washington, D.C.: National Academy Press.

Inselberg, R.M. (1962) Marital problems and satisfaction in high school marriages. *Marriage and Family Living* 24:74–77.

Kerckhoff, A.C., & Parrow, A.A. (1979) The effect of early marriage on the educational attainment of young men. *Journal of Marriage and the Family* 41:97–107.

Kinard, E.M., & Klerman, L.V. (1980) Teenage parenting and child abuse: Are they related? *American Journal of Orthopsychiatry* 50:481–88.

Kinard, E.M., & Reinherz, H. (1984) Behavioral and emotional functioning in children of adolescent mothers. *American Journal of Orthopsychiatry* 54:578–94.

Klerman, L. (1982) "Teenage parents: A brief review of research." In D.L. Parron & L. Eisenberg (eds.), *Infants at risk for developmental dysfunction,* pp. 125–32. Washington, D.C.: National Academy Press.

Lamb, M.E., & Elster, A.B. (1985) Adolescent mother-father relationships. *Developmental Psychology* 21:768–73.

Lorenzi, M.E., Klerman, L.V., & Jekel, J.F. (1977) School-age parents: How permanent a relationship? *Adolescence* 12:13–22.

Maracek, J. (1979) Psychological and behavioral status of children born to adolescent parents. Paper presented at the American Psychological Association, New York, New York.

McCarthy, J., & Menken, J. (1979) Marriage, remarriage, marital disruption and age at first birth. *Family Planning Perspectives* 11:21–30.

Nakashima, I.I., & Camp, B.W. (1984) Fathers of infants born to adolescent mothers. *American Journal of Diseases of Children* 138:452–54.

Nettleton, C.A., & Cline, D.W. (1975) Dating patterns, sexual relationships and use of contraceptives of 700 unwed mothers during a two-year period following delivery. *Adolescence* 37:45–57.

Nye, F.I., & Lamberts, M.B. (1980) *School-age parenthood: Consequences for babies, mothers, fathers, grandparents, and others.* Washington State University Cooperative Extension Bulletin 0667. Pullman, Washington: Washington State University.

Oates, R.K., Davis, A.A., Ryan, M.G., & Stewart, L.F. (1979) Risk factors associated with child abuse. *Child Abuse and Neglect* 3:547–53.

Rivara, F.P., Sweeney, P.J., & Henderson, B.F. (1986) Black teenage fathers: What happens when the child is born? *Pediatrics* 78:151–58.

Robinson, B.E., & Barret, R.L. (1986) *The developing father: Emerging roles in contemporary society.* New York: Guilford.

Roosa, M.W., Fitzgerald, H.E., & Carlson, N.A. (1982) A comparison of teenage and older mothers: A systems analysis. *Journal of Marriage and the Family* 44:367–77.

Rus-Eft, D., Sprenger, M., & Beever, H. (1979) Antecedents of adolescent parenthood and consequences at age 30. *The Family Coordinator* 28:173–79.

Scales, P., & Gordon, S. (1979) Preparing today's youth for tomorrow's family. *Journal of the Institute for Family Research and Education* 1:3–7.

Simkins, L. (1984) Consequences of teenage pregnancy and motherhood. *Adolescence* 19:39–54.

Stengel, R. (9 December 1985) The missing father myth. *Time:*90.

Unger, D.G., & Wandersman, L.P. (1985) Social support and adolescent mothers: Action research contributions to theory and application. *Journal of Social Issues* 41:29–45.

Welcher, D.W. (1982) "The effect of early childbearing on the psychosocial development of adolescent parents." In D.L. Parron & L. Eisenberg (eds.), *Infants at risk for developmental dysfunction*, pp. 115–23. Washington, D.C.: National Academy Press.

Wulf, D. (1986) Select committee says U.S. teenage pregnancy programs are neither effective nor comprehensive. *Family Planning Perspectives* 18:85–86.

Yogman, M.W. (1982) "Development of the father-infant relationship." In H.E. Fitzgerald, B.M. Lester, & M.W. Yogman (eds.), *Theory and research in behavioral pediatrics*, pp. 221–79. New York: Plenum Press.

Zuravin, S.J. (1987) Unplanned pregnancies, family planning problems, and child maltreatment. *Family Relations* 36:135–39.

4
Psychological Adjustment
of Teenage Fathers

It is not surprising that the father would show anxiety or depression
or fear or various conflicts under these conditions [out-of-wedlock
pregnancies]. To say on the basis of such evidence, however, that these
psychological states have contributed to the out-of-wedlock conception is a little bit like claiming that a study of a group of patients
whose appendixes had been removed showed that the cause of their
appendicitis was an abdominal scar.
                                        —Jerome Pauker (1971, p. 218)

*When my girlfriend told me she was pregnant, I wasn't really surprised. We'd
been dating for two years and had been having sex a lot for the past eight
months. Oh sure, we talked about protection and sometimes we used rub-
bers. But mostly we just liked sex without even thinking about a baby. We
talked about getting married after our senior year so the idea of a baby didn't
seem so awful. The night she told me she'd missed her period both of us were
scared. After talking about it we decided to go to a doctor in the next town
to find out if she was pregnant or not.*

*Once we found out Janie was really going to have a baby, we had to
make a decision. There was nobody I could talk to, so I pretty much stayed
by myself and worried. Even though things seemed to be closing in on me, I
dreamed about how fine things were going to be—how we'd get married and
about being a father. I knew it wouldn't be easy, but I could work at the mill
and we could live on my family's farm. I just knew we'd make it!*

*After hours of talking we decided to go to our parents, tell them every-
thing, and ask for their help. Graduation was two months off, and we
planned to get married then. Janie would only be four months along and
probably wouldn't be showing. Both of us had jobs; college would have to
be put off, but we felt we had made good—and realistic—plans. We went to
my parents first. Talking with them was hard because I knew I was really
letting them down. Mom cried and Dad mostly yelled at both of us. But after
lots of talk, they pretty much calmed down and agreed to think about our
plans.*

*Things at Janie's house were different. Her mom and dad both blew up—
and mostly at me! They refused to listen to anything we had to say and kept*

ing us how we let this happen and telling Janie what a no-good creep I s. Finally, after what seemed like hours, they told me to get out, so I left.

The next day Janie wasn't at school. As soon as classes ended, I went to her house to see what was going on. Her mom met me at the door and told me Janie was sick and needed to rest. She told me that this was normal and that Janie would call in a couple of days. Even though I didn't believe her, I didn't see that I had much choice. I worried a lot the next two days—I guess I knew something was wrong—and I was right!

Ater two days I went to Janie's and told her mom I wasn't leaving until I'd talked to Janie. Her dad came out and told me to get off their property and to never come back. He said they had taken her to a hospital where she had an abortion, and then she had gone to finish high school in another state! I couldn't believe it! I protested and tried to find Janie through her friends for weeks, but I never saw her again.

I felt put down by her family's lack of trust. Both of us had tried to be realistic and responsible. But her parents took all of that away from us, and I was robbed of my right to have some say-so in what would happen to my child. I don't think I'll ever get over it. *

Cliff, only 15 years old, had barely begun shaving when Sandy's pregnancy flung him, unprepared emotionally and financially, into parenthood with all its unfamiliar roles and responsibilities. While his friends talked mostly about upcoming soccer games and tests at school, he thought only about what he was going to do about Sandy and their baby. Cliff's situation is a true account of one boy's aloneness and fear of the sudden realization that he was about to be a father. He was a child entering the stark reality of an adult world with little support from society, friends, or even his family.

This chapter presents a descriptive profile of the teenage father's psychological adjustment to fatherhood. Based on research, the profile eliminates many of the old stereotypes of teen fathers as ruthless, unconcerned males only interested in their own sexual gratification. In contrast, it reveals frightened young men who are thrust into a highly conflicting and stressful situation and who cope by involving themselves, where permitted, in the fathering experience. The profile also shows that there are few differences between these young fathers and other teenage boys who have not fathered children or between teenage fathers and adult fathers.

---

*Reprinted with permission from B.E. Robinson and R.L. Barret (1986). *The developing father: Emerging roles in contemporary society.* New York: Guilford Press.

Stresses and Strains of Teenage Fatherhood

Research has revealed that expectant fathers have a wide range of emotions before, during, and after childbirth that were once believed to be exclusively maternal reactions (Flake-Hobson, Robinson, & Skeen 1983; Robinson & Barret 1986). We now know, for example, that many young men have the same emotional struggle and confusion that young mothers do (Robinson & Barret 1985). These emotions range from empathy and elation to depression. Teenage fathers not only experience the routine stresses of fatherhood, but an additional load of stresses and strains unique to adolescent parenthood.

Although we know that unwed teenage fathers are no different from other males on most measures of psychological functioning (Pauker 1971, Robinson & Barret 1987), a whole body of research suggests that the pregnancy-related stresses of teenage fatherhood frequently require counseling (Elster & Panzarine 1980, 1983; Fry & Trifiletti 1983; Hendricks 1980; Rothstein 1978). The literature suggests that stresses and anxieties of teenage fathers, although emanating from many sources, are developmental. The initial stress comes from knowledge of the pregnancy and premature role transition, decisions about the baby, and problems arising from the marital relationship (in cases where marriage occurs) and separation from the peer group.

Initial Knowledge and Premature Role Transition

The literature indicates that the teenage father's initial reaction, upon learning of his girlfriend's pregnancy, is directly correlated with how adequately he was coping with the pregnancy at the time of the interview (Elster & Panzarine 1980). Teenage fathers who had more difficulty coping with the pregnancy tended to be less well adjusted and to have a more negative initial reaction to the pregnancy. Seven out of the 16 unwed teen fathers in one study had difficulty coping with the pregnancy (43 percent), and six of these had signs of clinical depression and were referred for counseling (Elster & Panzarine 1980). Unwed teenage fathers in another study suffered depression and social isolation (Vaz, Smolen & Miller 1983). Reactions of being scared and mad were reported by 51 percent when they got news of the pregnancy, and 17 percent of this number said their negative reactions were mixed with feelings of happiness. Forty-one percent said they became depressed and 24 percent said they stopped going out with friends. Fully 75 percent of the twenty-six unwed expectant teenage fathers studied by Ouida Westney and her associates (1986) said they were not ready for fatherhood. They expressed a range of feelings, the most common being fear (46 percent). Other young men said they were sad, overwhelmed, shocked, or doubtful. Two-thirds of the respondents worried that the pregnancy would interfere with their future plans. One adolescent father told what it was like when he found out that his girlfriend was pregnant:

> I kinda got the feeling that it couldn't be true—I was just scared to death, didn't know what to do. Just a million things went through my mind. I was scared on the one hand having to consult my parents about the situation and then on the other hand I was kinda excited to know that I could be a father in nine months.

Although fatherhood is stressful at any age, teenagers have an even more traumatic time because of the premature role transition. Prospective fathers, having to deal not only with the worries of pregnancy but also with the stresses of normal adolescent development as well as the unscheduled developmental tasks of adulthood, face a triple developmental crisis. When they become fathers, young males essentially throw their lives off developmental kilter, as when they are bombarded by the developmental tasks of adolescence as well as those of adulthood. They either forego further education or attempt a "triple-track" pattern of undertaking education, work, and parenthood simultaneously, and in some cases they take on marriage as a fourth accelerated task (Russell 1980).

Sadler and Catrone (1983) further suggest that, not only are the developmental tasks of early parenthood added stressors for teenage parents, but they conflict with the developmental tasks of adolescence. According to this view, adolescence and parenthood occur along two separate developmental lines and both represent periods of dramatic growth, change, and potential turmoil:

> When these are superimposed it seems evident that there might be ample opportunity for the needs arising from one developmental process to conflict with those arising from the other. The potential for conflict appears to be most likely to occur when early parenthood occurs simultaneously with early adolescence. (p. 102)

The young father's role, for example, as a teenager, peer group member, high school student, or athlete may compete with his and society's role expectations of a father. Caparulo and London (1981) stress the need for guidance during this role conflict: "The young man who thinks he has all the answers about life, cars, girls—as an adolescent he has permission to be a know-it-all, difficult and inconsistent. All the answers about an infant's emotional, intellectual, physical development he really does not have and must listen to advice." (p. 32). This role conflict often leaves the teenager unprepared for fatherhood.

The case study of Cliff illustrates how adolescent fathers are frightened by what Fry and Trifiletti (1983) called "the undefined social territory into which they are stepping." Other accounts show that young fathers worry about the role conflict of being an adolescent and a father simultaneously and how this would affect their ability to be a good parent (Panzarine & Elster 1983):

> I've thought about it (fatherhood) a lot, and it scares me. Hell, I'll admit it—I'm not a full grown man and I never try to pretend to be. I'm still, well, a child in a sense . . . I'll love it, but I'm not sure I'll know how to teach it and guide it. (p. 119)

Some social scientists found that the abrupt role change from teenage boy to teenage father shortens the time span for the gradual accomplishment of the heterosexual social maturational process and places teenage fathers at psychiatric risk (Fry & Trifilleti 1983). These boys experienced high levels of emotional rejection, personal anxiety, as well as feelings of self-blame and guilt. Rejection feelings were perceived as especially strong from the girl-friend's parents and peers. Isolation from peers is especially painful at a time when the peer group is essential in personality development. The teenage father got little support from his peers, and if he tried to talk about his fears, was told to keep cool by his friends (Fry & Trifiletti 1983).

Decisions about the Baby

After the initial shock wears off, one of the greatest stressors is being left in the dark when decisions are made about the father's baby, primarily by the mother and her parents, without his input. Vaz, Smolen, and Miller (1983) found that one-half of the teen mothers and fathers in their study disagreed over whether or not the male helped with the decisions about keeping the baby. Although 53 percent of the mothers felt their partners had input, only 49 percent of the males believed they had helped with the decision. This finding suggests that a gap in communication exists between partners over a critical aspect of the pregnancy and that males may not be as much a part of decision as other parties believe.

Feedback from adolescent fathers revealed that, although frightened, they wanted to become involved and to contribute to decision-making and planning concerning their female partners and babies (Barret & Robinson 1982, Fry & Trifiletti 1983). Teenage fathers often are not told when the baby is born or that their children have been adopted or turned over to foster care (Robinson & Barret 1985). Consider Dave (see chapter 1) who, refusing to go home after the birth of his son, struggled alone in the hospital waiting room with the reality of giving up his baby. Or Cliff, who felt robbed because he could not participate in the fate of his own child.

Redmond (1985) found that most of the teen fathers she studied wanted to be an integral part of decisions regarding their offspring. In fact, she found that the more the adolescent male is involved in the decision-making process, the more active he is during and after the pregnancy:

> Most males wish to be included in this decision-making process and receive emotional and social support during this time. When not included, they feel confused and neglected. These feelings may create problems for their girlfriends and professionals in obtaining a smooth resolution and outcome of the pregnancy (Redmond 1985, p. 342)

Other social scientists found that the greatest rejection experienced by teenage fathers occurred in cases where babies were aborted (Fry & Trifiletti 1983). Data indicate that teenage fathers do not endorse the practice of abortion for their partners "because it is wrong" (Hendricks 1982). In abortion situations male partners seldom, if ever, participate in the decision to abort the baby or give it up for adoption. This set of circumstances was found to intensify anxiety and rejection that the males were already experiencing.

The words of a 17-year-old waiting while his girlfriend had an abortion are typical of the emotional conflict of teenage fathers:

> I thought I was a much more liberated man. I'd be able to walk in here and sit down and say, "here's an abortion," and that would be it. But now that I'm here, I'm a wreck. . . . How about me? Do they have something for me to lay on while I die? (Rothstein 1978, p. 208).

When Cliff found out that Sandy's parents had taken her to a nearby town for an abortion and had sent her to another state to live with relatives, he stammered, tears flowing down his cheeks, at the overwhelming feelings of isolation and rejection: "I couldn't believe it! Sometimes I get real angry that nobody asked me what I thought needed to be done."

Marriage and Early Parenthood

There is sufficient evidence to suggest that marriage assuages some of the role ambiguities associated with unwed adolescent fatherhood and reduces the stress levels. Perhaps marriage provides role clarification to the sudden state of affairs. Fry and Trifiletti (1983) found in their study of thirty-five married and sixty unmarried adolescent fathers, that fathers who married or planned to marry felt less stress, anxiety, and rejection than unwed fathers. Married fathers were more confident about their responsibilities to themselves and others, compared to unmarried fathers, who felt uncertain in their roles towards themselves as parent, towards the baby, and toward the happiness of the girlfriend. Married subjects also showed less guilt and were less self-blaming (as when they blamed themselves for involving the girlfriend in sex and making her pregnant) than unmarried males. Despite differences between married and unmarried teen fathers, however, marriage is not the solution to teen pregnancy and is not without its own stresses. A 19-year-old father, for example, confessed:

> One of the stresses I have is having to make sure I can provide for my family and feed them and buy all the diapers and everything I need and make sure I have the money for them to take care of all that. The strain is the sleep I lose at night from hearing the babies cry. I've always been one that needs a lot of sleep, and I just don't get that much anymore. I get up, go to work from 8:00 until 5:30, come home and try to relieve my wife with some of the duties with the babies. I don't do too much, but I do try to help her out a little bit. Then I mainly just eat supper, read a few stories to my kids, and go to bed. I miss going out with the guys and a lot of my friends. But then I don't worry about who's got the party and where's everybody going. I know where I'm going to be at night now—at home. And that takes a lot of pressure off you in some ways.

Interviews from a group of twenty teenage fathers, who had married by the time of delivery, identified four major stressors during gestation and early parenthood (Elster & Panzarine 1983):

> *Vocational-educational concerns* centered around how they would financially support their new families and around not finishing school or getting and maintaining a job.

> *Health concerns* included worries about the mother's health and future welfare of mother and baby.

> *Parenting concerns* dealt with their performance in terms of disciplining and caring for their children.

> *Relationship concerns* had to do with their relationships with their partners, parents, friends, and feelings of alienation from the church.

The authors of the study found that the stressors on these young fathers changed in intensity throughout pregnancy and the early postnatal period. But because of their ages and truncated schooling, all the young fathers worried that they were not financially able to support a family. This concern remained elevated at each interview interval. The greatest concern at the third trimester interview was vocational-educational concerns, expressed by 100 percent of the teens, followed by health concerns for 94 percent. Relationship concerns followed (76 percent), and parenting concerns were cited as the least stressor (35 percent).

Hendricks (1980) also reported that the twenty teen fathers in his study worried about financial responsibilities, parenting skills, education, employment, transportation, relationships with girlfriends, and facing life in general. Similar stresses were cited in a more recent follow-up study of eighty-one teen fathers (Rivara, Sweeney, and Henderson 1986). The most commonly mentioned problems were finances, finding a job, not being able to see the baby often enough, and relationship troubles with the mother of the child. These young fathers believed that the services needed most by adolescent fathers were job training (50 percent) and counseling (22 percent). Education in child care was also perceived as important.

Coping Strategies and Early Involvement

The early literature from maternal reports indicated that 50 percent of teenage males cope with fatherhood by abandoning their partners after the pregnancy (Babikian & Goldman 1971). Contrary to the stereotype that unwed teenage fathers disappear at the first mention of pregnancy, more recent and better designed studies indicate that it is the young fathers who have been abandoned—pushed away by social agencies, peers, and the adolescent mother's family. We now know that the fathers will become deeply involved when permitted, and that it is the exclusion from the fathering and decision-making process that causes stress among these young men. In fact, the literature shows that it is through involvement that young fathers deal with their stress and learn to cope with impending fatherhood.

Findings from twenty teen fathers who volunteered to participate in an exploratory study unearthed ten coping strategies in their transition to fatherhood (Panzarine & Elster 1983). All ten strategies included the teenager's involvement as opposed to his flight from the responsibilities of parenthood.

> All twenty fathers assumed the role of provider by engaging in some direct action to improve their financial situation. Some who were unemployed found jobs whereas others left school to work full time.

> Ninety percent of the fathers helped prepare for the baby. This strategy included buying baby clothes, supplies, or toys, or helping prepare the infant's room.

> Seventy percent of the young fathers coped by talking with others about impending fatherhood. Talks with their partners, friends, or parents about the fathering role helped them clarify their responsibilities regarding child care and household tasks. Information-seeking from their own fathers about what being a father was like provided reassurance from those who had already been through the experience.

Only 20 percent of the young men used observation and evaluation of other people's interactions with children as a coping mechanism. They seemed to use these experiences to identify behavior they wanted to either emulate or avoid.

Another 20 percent read pamphlets given them by the hospital and purchased books on fatherhood and child care so they would know what to expect in their new role.

Sixty percent of the teen fathers said they fantasized about fatherhood and the baby and daydreamed of being in different situations with their children, outlining the kinds of things they would teach them.

Thirty-five percent of the youths reflected about how they had been reared and began to evalute their parents' parenting abilities.

Thirty percent said their expectant father role had made them settle down, and they had ended their partying, drinking, and fighting. They reported that contacts with single friends had been replaced with friendships with married peers. The authors interpreted this behavior as a mobilization of "an intrapsychic process" to reduce the emotional discomfort accompanying loss of peer contact.

Ten percent resorted to alcohol abuse to deal with their ambivalence over becoming a father.

Fifteen percent avoided thinking ahead about fatherhood or the baby and denied that the baby might have an impact on their lives.

My own work and that of my colleague, Dr. Robert Barret, with teenage fathers verified their frustrations about being omitted from decisions. For many, the pregnancies were their first opportunities to function in the adult world. Being exluded only increased their sense of alienation and helplessness (Barret & Robinson 1986).

Teenage Fathers versus Teenage Nonfathers

There is widespread belief that adolescent fathers are psychologically inferior to adolescent males in general and to fathers in general. This belief was generated by early attempts to explain such unconventional actions by these youth. The adolescent father, who supposedly had difficulty with his sexual identity, was said to resolve the conflict by impregnating an adolescent female, thereby proving his masculinity (Pannor, Massarik, & Evans 1971; Vincent 1956). Since these early reports, numerous studies have compared adolescent fathers with their nonfather agemates and with adult fathers. Findings from these studies have gradually dispelled the early myth.

As box 4–1 indicates, few differences between teenage fathers and teenage boys who have not fathered children emerge from the research. Studies where teenage males are matched by age and other demographic factors show some attitudinal and background differences between fathers and nonfathers in terms of contraception and adolescent pregnancy. However, teen fathers and nonfathers were no different on either sexual knowledge and behavior or standardized psychological measures.

One of the earliest studies on attitudes toward conception and pregnancy compared twenty-two unwed adolescent fathers with twenty-two unwed nonfathers, all of whom were wards of the California Youth Authority (Robbins & Lynn 1973). Each boy participated in a sixty-minute interview. Fathers differed significantly from nonfathers on their views about illegitimacy. Teen fathers were more likely to approve of their children's becoming unwed parents, approve of extramarital sex, disapprove of contraceptives, marry a woman with an illegitimate child by another man, and believe that their offspring would not be affected by their behavior. Fathers also came from backgrounds that seemed more conducive to unwed pregnancies. That is, the young fathers were more likely to be illegitimate themselves, have a sibling who was born out of wedlock, and have a sibling who was an unwed parent.

Redmond's (1985) Canadian study of adolescent male attitudes toward pregnancy and fatherhood also yielded differences between fathers and nonfathers. Fathers were more likely than nonfathers to believe that teens should be allowed to get an abortion, to accompany the girl for an abortion, and to give emotional support after an abortion.

A comparison of 100 adolescent fathers with 100 nonfathers revealed more similarities than differences between the two groups (Rivara, Sweeney & Henderson 1985). For example, there were no differences in self-image or personality adjustment between the two groups of adolescents. In addition, there were no differences between frequency of sexual intercourse during the preceding year—both having had sex several times a month. Knowledge of sex, pregnancy, and contraception between groups was also equivalent—both fathers and nonfathers were basically uninformed. No differences emerged between groups in the perceived effectiveness of pregnancy prevention by various contraceptives, and both groups often had unprotected intercourse.

The only notable difference was that teenage fathers were significantly more likely to accept teenage pregnancy in their families as a common occurrence, minimally disruptive to their current and future lives. The fact that these results show that teenage fathers perceive adolescent fatherhood as a normative cultural experience may account for the absence of anxiety or poor self-concept found in some studies (Robinson & Barret 1987).

Box 4-1
Studies Showing Similarities and Differences Between Teenage Fathers (TFs) and Teenage Nonfathers (TNs)

Similarities	*Differences*

Attitudes

• Child development knowledge and attitudes (Rivara, Sweeney & Henderson 1986)	• TFs more permissive in their views toward illegitimacy (Robbins & Lynn 1973) • TFs more likely to accept teenage pregnancy in their families (Rivara, Sweeney & Henderson 1985) • TFs more liberal in their attitudes toward abortion (Redmond 1985)

Background

	• TFs more likely to be born out of wedlock (McCoy & Tyler 1985; Robbins & Lynn 1973)

Sexual Knowledge and Behavior

• Frequency of sexual intercourse (Rivara, Sweeney & Henderson 1985) • Knowledge of sex, pregnancy, and contraception (Rivara, Sweeney & Henderson 1985) • Perceived effectiveness of contraceptives (Rivara, Sweeney & Henderson 1985)	

Psychological Variables

• Locus of control (McCoy & Tyler 1985; Robinson, Barret & Skeen 1983) • Personality adjustment (Rivara, Sweeney & Henderson 1985) • Interpersonal trust (McCoy & Tyler 1985) • Self-image (Rivara, Sweeney & Henderson 1985) • Coping style (McCoy & Tyler 1985) • Intellectual functioning (Pauker 1971) • Mood, depression, and anxiety levels (Rivara, Sweeney & Henderson 1986)	• TFs more active and less controlled (Pauker 1971)

Follow-up interviews on this sample eighteen months later generally revealed few differences between teen fathers and nonfathers on a number of factors (Rivara, Sweeney & Henderson 1986). Both, for instance, had higher expectations of their infants than were developmentally appropriate. At nine months both groups had inadequate knowledge of child development and child health maintenance. At eighteen months, though, significantly more nonfathers knew the normal development and normal diet of a newborn than did fathers. In addition, standardized measurements indicated that fathers had no greater alterations of mood or greater depression and anxiety than the nonfathers.

An important study by Pauker (1971) was based on the premise that many reports of psychological maladjustment among teenage fathers occur because data are assessed *after* the traumatic out-of-wedlock experience. His approach was to compare intelligence and psychological test scores of ninety-four teenage boys (between ages 13 and 19) *before* they had fathered a child and ninety-four teenage boys (matched by age) who had never fathered a child. The boys scored identically on the standardized intelligence tests. Moreover, the differences on the Minnesota Multiphasic Personality Inventory were negligible, but those that were significant might suggest that the unwed fathers were somewhat more active and less controlled than the nonfathers. However, the researcher did not interpret this difference as negative or in any way reinforcing the old stereotype of unwed fathers. In contrast, he emphasized the fact that on the majority of the thirteen scales, overlap of the two group's scores was extensive.

Two other studies, dealing with inner control between groups of teen fathers versus nonfathers, found no differences (McCoy & Tyler 1985; Robinson, Barret, and Skeen 1983). Robinson and his associates (1983) administered the Nowicki-Strickland Locus of Control Scale to twenty unwed adolescent fathers and twenty matched-for-age nonfathers. The investigators reported that the two groups obtained equivalent scores on the measures. They concluded that adolescent fathers do not suffer from the inability to control their sexual urges any more than their nonfather contemporaries.

A later study, comparing twenty-four unwed adolescent fathers and twenty-seven unwed adolescent nonfathers between the ages of 15 and 19, corroborated these findings (McCoy & Tyler 1985). No differences were found between groups on their belief in a sense of personal control and responsibility for their own lives (as assessed by the Notter Internal-External Locus of Control Scale). Moreover, fathers and nonfathers were not significantly different in interpersonal trust or coping styles. Teenage fathers did, however, tend to be older and were more likely to be born out of wedlock.

Teenage Fathers versus Adult Fathers

A teen father, I'll call him Lester, rationalized the advantages of being a young father at 17, compared to a first-time father in his twenties:

> I would much rather be a young father than an older father because there's a lot of sleepless nights. And I believe if I was too much older I couldn't handle the daytime at work and school and everything at home. When they [kids] get a little older and I'm not so old, I'll have a chance to have a lot more in common with them than if I was say 65 when they turn 15—they'd be walking me around in a wheelchair. Maybe now when I'm 30 and they're 15, I'll get to play a little basketball with them.

Lester's personal views about the father's age raises important questions surrounding adolescent pregnancy. Are there sufficient differences between teen fathers (19 and below) and adult fathers (20 and above) who have adolescent partners that warrant their distinction in the literature? As box 4–2 indicates, the similarities far outweigh the differences in studies designed to examine possible age distinctions.

Several studies were designed to examine possible age differences. Nakashima and Camp (1984) studied thirty-five fathers with adolescent partners, divided into two groups: twenty teenage fathers were age 19 or younger (the

Box 4–2
Studies Showing Similarities and Differences Between Teenage Fathers (TFs) and Adult Fathers (AFs)

Similarities	*Differences*
Attitudes	
• Attitudes toward childrearing (Nakashima & Camp 1984) • Perceived marital relationship (Lamb & Elster 1985)	• AFs perceived less marital conflict than TFs (Nakashima & Camp 1984)
Psychological Variables	
• Self-image (Robinson & Barret 1987) • Stress/anxiety (Lamb & Elster 1985; Robinson & Barret 1987) • Intellectual functioning (Nakashima & Camp 1984) • Social support (Lamb & Elster 1985)	

young-young group) and fifteen adult fathers were 20 years of age or older (the young-old group). A third group of sixteen older fathers age 20 or older (the old-old group) and married to adult mothers were also studied for comparison.

All fathers were asked to complete questionnaires providing demographic information and several standardized instruments measuring parental attitudes. Findings showed that, with the exception of marital conflict, teenage and adult partners of adolescent girls had similar characteristics. Older partners of adolescent girls perceived less marital conflict than the other two groups of men. The authors conjectured that teen parents were less likely to compromise and more likely to be immature and less concerned with others' needs. Unrealistic expectations of the relationship may not allow it to survive the disappointment.

Older men paired with older partners had more education and better vocabularies. Perhaps the more important finding, however, was that the similarities between teenage fathers and adult fathers are greater than the differences. Both groups were similar in their hostile/controlling attitudes, childrearing philosophies, and in their intellectual functioning. The older man who paired with an adolescent girl was more like the adolescent father than he was like the older man who paired with an older woman.

A later study (Lamb & Elster 1985) also addressed the father's age as an influence on the adolescent-mother-infant-father relationship. A total of fifty-one males were divided into three groups: eighteen fathers were 19.5 years of age or below; seventeen adult partners were between 19.6 and 22 years of age; and sixteen adult men were between 22.2 and 29.9 years of age. Fathers, mothers, and infants were observed interacting at home for forty minutes. Following the observations, fathers completed several questionnaires.

No differences were derived among the different age groups of fathers in regard to interactions with their infants, reported stress, social support, and perceived quality of marital relationship. The findings on perceived marital relationships conflict with that of Nakashima and Camp (1984), who found greater perceived marital discord among teen fathers than adult partners of adolescent girls.

A third study compared twelve teenage fathers (between 16 and 18 years of age) and twelve adult fathers (21 years of age or more) on self-concept and anxiety (Robinson & Barret 1987). Scores on the Personal Attribute Inventory (self-concept measure) and the Stait-Trait Anxiety Scale (anxiety measure) were similar for both groups.

The nonsignificant findings on self-concept and anxiety level between adolescent and adult fathers follow a pattern of nonsignificant differences in the literature. Box 4–2 shows that, with the exception of perceived marital conflict, teen fathers and adult men who father children by adolescent females are similar in attitudes and psychological functioning. This trend, how-ever, should not be interpreted to mean that teenage boys are more like adult men, especially since the review here and elsewhere also suggests that teenage fathers are actually more like their teenage nonfather counterparts. A more likely interpretation was stated by Nakashima and Camp (1984): "The re-semblance of the older man who chooses an adolescent partner to the adoles-cent father was so consistent that it supports the clinical impression of inade-quacy in the older man who chooses the adolescent woman and raises the question of developmental arrest in these men." (p. 454)

Conclusion

The adjustment of adolescent males to fatherhood is a difficult process. Al-though biologically men, teen fathers are boys in almost every other respect. They are as uninformed about sex as other teenage boys and are emotionally and intellectually unprepared for parenthood. Their premature role transi-tion causes stresses and strains that compound tensions already inherent in adolescence.

Additional pressures occur in regard to decisions about the baby, prob-lems in marriage, and separation from the peer group. Most young men want to participate in the fathering experience and, when permitted, become in-volved as one means of adjusting to the role of fatherhood.

Despite the difficulties of adjusting to teenage parenthood, unwed fathers are no different psychologically from adolescent boys in general or from adult men who father babies by adolescent females. On the contrary, they are simi-lar in self-image, intellectual functioning, locus of control, personality adjust-ment, interpersonal trust, coping style, social support, and anxiety and mood. Although psychologically normal, adolescent fathers lack knowledge about sexuality, conception, and child development as do other adolescent males with whom they have been compared. Young fathers also seem to be less concerned than young nonfathers regarding the consequences of preg-nancy and abortion and are more likely to be born out of wedlock them-selves. Although young fathers' attitudes toward childrearing and perceptions of marital relationships are equivalent to that of older fathers, there is some indication that adult fathers perceive less marital conflict than teenage fa-thers.

References

Babikian, H.M., & Goldman, A. (1971) A study of teenage pregnancy. *American Journal of Psychiatry* 128:755–60.

Barret, R.L., & Robinson, B.E. (1982) A descriptive study of teenage expectant fathers. *Family Relations* 31:349–52.
———. (1986) Adolescent fathers: Often forgotten parents. *Pediatric Nursing* 2:273–77.
Caparulo, F., & London, K. (1981) Adolescent fathers: Adolescents first, fathers second. *Issues in Health Care of Women* 3:23–33.
Elster, A.B., & Panzarine, S. (1980) Unwed teenage fathers: Emotional and health educational needs. *Journal of Adolescent Health Care* 1:116–20.
———. (1983) Teenage fathers: Stresses during gestation and early parenthood. *Clinical Pediatrics* 22:700–703.
Flake-Hobson, C., Robinson, B.E., & Skeen, P. (1983) *Child development and relationships*. New York: Random House.
Fry, P.S., & Trifiletti, R.J. (1983) Teenage fathers: An exploration of their developmental needs and anxieties and the implications for clinical-social intervention services. *Journal of Psychiatric Treatment and Evaluation* 5:219–27.
Hendricks, L.E. (1980) Unwed adolescent fathers: Problems they face and their sources of social support. *Adolescence* 15:861–69.
———. (1982) Unmarried black adolescent fathers' attitudes toward abortion, contraception, and sexuality: A preliminary report. *Journal of Adolescent Health Care* 2:199–203.
Lamb, M.E., & Elster, A.B. (1985) Adolescent mother-infant-father relationships. *Developmental Psychology* 21:768–73.
McCoy, J.E., & Tyler, F.B. (1985) Selected psychosocial characteristics of black unwed adolescent fathers. *Journal of Adolescent Health Care* 6:12–16.
Nakashima, I.I., & Camp, B.W. (1984) Fathers of infants born to adolescent mothers. *American Journal of Diseases of Children* 138:452–54.
Pannor, R., Massarik, F., & Evans, B. (1971) *The unmarried father: New approaches for helping unmarried young parents*. New York: Springer.
Panzarine, S., & Elster, A.B. (1983) Coping in a group of expectant adolescent fathers: An exploratory study. *Journal of Adolescent Health Care* 4:117–20.
Pauker, J.D. (1971) Fathers of children conceived out of wedlock: Pregnancy, high school, psychological test results. *Developmental Psychology* 4:215–18.
Redmond, M.A. (1985) Attitudes of adolescent males toward adolescent pregnancy and fatherhood. *Family Relations* 34:337–42.
Rivara, F.P., Sweeney, P.J., & Henderson, B.F. (1985) A study of low socioeconomic status, black teenage fathers and their nonfather peers. *Pediatrics* 75:648–56.
Rivara, F.P., Sweeney, P.J., & Henderson, B.F. (1986) Black teenage fathers: What happens when the child is born? *Pediatrics* 78:151–58.
Robbins, M.M., & Lynn, D. (1973) The unwed fathers: Generation recidivism and attitudes about intercourse in California Youth Authority wards. *Journal of Sex Research* 9:334–41.
Robinson, B.W., & Barret, R.L. (1985, December) Teenage fathers. *Psychology Today* 19:66–70.
———. (1986) *The developing father: Emerging roles in contemporary society*. New York: Guilford.
———. (1987) Self-concept and anxiety of adolescent and adult fathers. *Adolescence*. In press.

Robinson, B.E., Barret, R.L., & Skeen, P. (1983) Locus of control of unwed adolescent fathers versus adolescent nonfathers. *Perceptual and Motor Skills* 56:397–98.

Rothstein, A.A. (1978) Adolescent males, fatherhood, and abortion. *Journal of Youth and Adolescence* 7:203–214.

Russell, C.S. (1980) Unscheduled parenthood: Transition to "parent" for the teenager. *Journal of Social Issues* 36:46–63.

Sadler, L.S., & Catrone, C. (1983) The adolescent parent: A dual developmental crisis. *Journal of Adolescent Health Care* 4:100–105.

Vaz, R., Smolen, P., & Miller, C. (1983) Adolescent pregnancy: Involvement of the male partner. *Journal of Adolescent Health Care* 4:246–50.

Vincent, C. (1956) *Unwed mothers.* New York: The Free Press.

Westney, O.E., Cole, O.J., & Munford, T.L. (1986) Adolescent unwed prospective fathers: Readiness for fatherhood and behaviors toward the mother and the expected infant. *Adolescence* 21:901–11.

5
Problems in Studying Teenage Fathers

> All eyes are on the unwed mother and her baby, while the other part-
> ner stands awkwardly in the background, too often ignored or even
> forgotten completely.
>
> —Lisa Connolly (1978, p. 40)

*Distinguished researchers and medical experts convened in 1982 at a confer-
ence of the Division of Mental Health, Institute of Medicine. Among the
many sessions on adolescent pregnancy and parenthood, the teenage father
was barely mentioned. When he was discussed, he was portrayed as the stereotypical villainous stud.*

> *The reaction of the adolescent father to a pregnancy and child was men-
> tioned briefly. Although data are scanty, some boys view a girl's pregnancy
> as a sign of their sexual competence, and for those who are disadvantaged,
> this may be perceived as one of the few successful achievements in their lives.
> In addition, a boy's peer group may identify him as "being a stud," and the
> boy may feel a heightened motivation to impregnate the same or another
> girl again. A differing reaction, however, may take place. . . . a small pro-
> portion of men have feelings of conflict when they become fathers, and their
> hostility may be directed outwards. Although this type of study has not been
> done on teenage fathers, there may be a percentage of boys who act out
> their emotions in violent or quasi-violent ways. More information on the
> father's feelings and motivations would add to an understanding of the ado-
> lescent mother. (Harrison 1982, p. 49)*

These conference proceedings imply that researchers and medical scholars
see teenage fathers as secondary in importance to the female partner and
worthy of research only as a means to a better understanding of the adolescent mother. Although some young fathers may fit the stereotype presented
at the conference, it is surprising, yet understandable, that well-intentioned
researchers continue to draw conclusions that have never been scientifically
corroborated. This chapter shows problems researchers face in studying teenage fathers and how unsubstantiated beliefs are routinely accepted in the absence of solid facts.

Empirical Neglect

As with any new area of study, teenage fatherhood has received little empirical attention, presumably because young fathers are a difficult population to reach (Barret & Robinson 1982). Another reason, however, is the overall neglect of the role of fathers in the family and parenting literature (Robinson & Barret 1986). Margaret Mead's famous comment that "fathers are a biological necessity but a social accident" accurately described the limited role expected of men in families. This pervasive view resulted in the role of the father as unimportant in his offspring's development. The slighting of all areas of fatherhood in the literature led one sociologist to characterize most family studies as *wives sociology* (Safilios-Rothschild 1969). This term, or one similar to it, *partner's sociology* perhaps, appropriately characterizes the literature on teenage parenthood.

Throughout the 1960s and 1970s, research on teenage parenting largely ignored fathers (Barret & Robinson 1981, Chilman 1979, Earls & Siegel 1980). Even today when the term *adolescent parenthood* is used, the reference is almost exclusively adolescent mothers. Titles of articles and books (for example, "adolescent pregnancy" or "teenage parenting") would seem to suggest that both mothers and fathers are covered. In fact, fathers continue to appear only rarely in these reports. Almost thirty years ago, Vincent (1960) cited the ratio of studies of unmarried fathers to studies of unwed mothers to be one to twenty-five. In the early 1980s, an analysis of a series of studies revealed that in 30 percent of the cases, the rubrics referred exclusively to adolescent mothers (Robinson & Barret 1982).

Some examples include Babikian and Goldman's (1971) study on adolescent pregnancy which included thirty adolescent mothers but not one father. Zelnik and Kantner (1972, 1979) surveyed a national sample of 4,600 females between 15 and 19 years old regarding incidences of sexuality, contraception, and pregnancy. Adolescent males were once more excluded.

Scott, Field, and Robertson (1980) preface their book, *Teenage Parents and Their Offspring,* with: "This book is and was born out of concern about the outcome from teenage pregnancies for the mother and infant." A 1980 special issue of the *American Journal of Orthopsychiatry* dealt with teenage pregnancy. Only one out of seven of those articles addressed adolescent fatherhood.

During the 1970s, however, the tides began to turn during what one researcher called "the age of paternal rediscovery" (Lamb 1979). A flood of fathering research followed and during the 1980s a series of books emerged on fatherhood that covered every possible fathering role from traditional fathers to never-married single and adoptive fathers, divorced fathers, stepfathers, gay fathers, fathers of disabled children, and adolescent fathers (Hanson & Bozett 1985, Robinson & Barret 1986). Although this trend is encouraging, the quantity and quality of research has not kept up with the demand for more information. This is particularly true for the area of adolescent fatherhood, one of the last father role frontiers to be explored.

Inferential Sources of Information

History has repeated itself through the research on teenage fathers. Many of the same methodological shortcomings made in the pioneer studies on fathers in general have been made with adolescent fathers. For example, the majority of data on teenage fathers ironically have been inferred from populations that contain no teen fathers. Generalizations regarding the adolescent father's contraceptive knowledge, attitudes toward pregnancy, and behavior in terms of pregnancy have been drawn from practically every source except that of the teenage father: maternal interviews, adolescent fathers subsumed within a larger population of older unmarried fathers, antecedent studies conducted on teenagers *before* they become fathers, and adolescent males who are not necessarily teenage fathers (Barret & Robinson 1986).

Maternal Interviews

The maternal interview is a notorious practice that has led to biased views in the parenting and fatherhood literature (LeMasters & DeFrain 1983, Robinson & Barret 1986). This practice has, unfortunately, been adopted by some researchers of teen fathers and has led to serious methodological flaws in the literature (Barret & Robinson 1982). Earls and Siegel (1980) noted that:

> Since pregnancy may in many cases be socially stigmatized, the stress associated with the experience can produce distortion of interview data, particularly if it is limited to questionnaires, which may result in a negative bias in describing the father's role. It is remarkable that, in several papers reviewed, no mention was made of this source of bias nor was the desirability of directly interviewing fathers ever discussed. (p. 471).

Few studies cite this practice as a limitation or note that direct father contact would have been a methodological improvement.

One example of how maternal interviews can conceal or distort the facts was presented by Platts (1968), who reported instances in which teenage mothers informed caseworkers that their relationship with their child's father had ended, when they had actually tried to protect the father from being harassed by the agency. Another study, employing maternal interviews to discern the degree of permanency in the relationship, reported that social workers' questions about the "putative" father were frequently met with hositility or lack of cooperation from the adolescent mothers (Lorenzi, Klerman & Jekel 1977). Other reports indicate that young mothers often feel betrayed and alone and refuse to identify the father until they have worked through their own feelings (Allen-Meares 1984).

The validity of maternal reports is called into question since an embittered mother may unwittingly or deliberately portray her husband or estranged boyfriend in an unfavorable light to gain sympathy for herself. Or she may want to protect the father and make him appear more responsible and involved than he really is. Moreover, the exclusion of adolescent fathers from research seems to support Mead's old adage as well as to imply that these young men are dispensable in the parenting process and that mothers are reliable sources regarding the nature of teenage fathers' feelings and thoughts. Surprisingly, reliance on adolescent maternal samples in lieu of teen fathers has continued into the 1980s. In one study researchers used children's names—that is, whether or not children were named after their fathers—as a clue to the adolescent father's actual and symbolic importance in the kinship system (Furstenberg & Talvitie 1980). Even in their attempt to highlight the teen father, these researchers relied on secondhand reports derived from interviews with teenage mothers—a practice to which they resorted with some misgivings because "most males simply could not be located without an inordinate amount of time and expense" (p. 37).

A later study used interviews with thirty adolescent mothers to assess childrearing practices, family support, and support from the social network as they pertained to fatherhood (Gershenson 1983). The following excerpt is a sample of the kinds of interpretations that were drawn from the teen mother's perspective of her husband:

> The mothers tended to find the fathers too strict, although the conception of too strict varied greatly from household to household. None of the mothers felt that there were serious disagreements about discipline; their husbands simply tended to be less understanding. (p. 593)

It was unclear and surprising that the fathers were never interviewed, especially since the study dealt with redefining fatherhood. We have known for some time that parental interviews yield significantly different versions of childrearing from maternal ones (Mueller 1970, Seeley 1956). Recent evidence further indicates that teenage fathers, although difficult to reach, are accessible (Barret & Robinson 1987). Many times this involves going beyond the mother and often through her as a link to the father.

Older Unmarried Fathers

Studies in which teen fathers are subsumed within larger samples of older unmarried fathers cloud our knowledge of the adolescent population since data are not pulled out so that a profile of young fathers can be drawn (for example, Leashore 1979, Lerman 1986, Pfuhl 1978, Rothstein 1978, Vincent 1960). In many of these instances it is difficult to know the numbers of teen fathers and to interpret the results separately from the older unmarried men.

Clark Vincent (1960) conducted one of the earliest and largest sociological studies of 201 unmarried fathers, and for that reason alone, this study is important. Vincent's analysis was also significant because it countered the popular notion that unwed fathers are sexual exploiters of young, naive females. A major drawback, however, was that only slightly more than 15 percent were 18 years of age or younger and they were lumped with older fathers, which made it difficult to know how much of the findings apply to teenage males.

Another sociologist, Erdwin Pfuhl (1978), studied 140 unwed fathers, a sample which contained 64 adolescent fathers. He examined the label *deviant* to see how unwed fathers viewed the label as applicable to them. Although the males acknowledged their behavior as rule violating, they did not identify themselves as deviant. Yet since data were not analyzed separately by age, it is impossible to know how or if adolescent fathers differed from their older counterparts in these attitudes.

In his review of research, Leashore (1979) recommends a need for more systematic and representative research regarding unmarried fathers. Characteristics of each study—such as sample size and variables selected for study—make comparisons between them difficult and questionable. Leashore also concluded that a significant number of teen fathers are included in the unmarried father category in these studies.

The most illustrative case is the widely circulated book by Pannor, Massarik, and Evans (1971). In their preface, the authors suggest that a main goal is to help teen fathers: "While the young mother can often assume her role as wife and mother with relative ease, the teenage father is much less frequently prepared for the responsibilities of being a husband and father. We must provide him with help so that becoming responsible can, indeed, be an attainable objective." (p. xi). Tagged as the first comprehensive study purporting to discern more information about teenage fathers, the Vista Del Mar study was not about teen fathers at all. Although a majority of unmarried mothers in the study were adolescent (57 percent), most of the fathers (71.6 percent) ranged in age from 20 to over 40 years. In fact, only twenty-eight of the ninety-six unmarried fathers were actually under 19 years of age. Despite this fact, later writers grossly misinterpreted the data and conveyed the message that the study dealt exclusively with teenage males. Connolly (1978), for example said, "The study [the Vista Del Mar study] concerned itself with a small population of primarily middle-class Jewish boys" (p. 42). And Fry and Trifiletti (1983) reported, "The Vista Del Mar Study demonstrated for the first time the intense developmental anxieties of boy-fathers" (p. 220).

A recent national study was performed by Lerman (1986), who scrutinized data from the National Longitudinal Survey (NLS) to establish a profile of the young absent father. Unfortunately, his study had two major drawbacks. First, the NLS oversampled blacks, Hispanics, and poor whites, the end result being a greater number of young absent fathers than would have resulted from a representative national sample. Second, his definition of "young" was the wide age span of 14 to 21 years old, which dilutes the teen father category.

Developmentally, age is a distinguishing factor in characterizing unmarried fathers, as the denotation *teenage father* indicates. It has been suggested that the premature role transition to fatherhood results in young fathers experiencing more stresses than men who are developmentally prepared for fatherhood (Elster & Panzarine 1983). Teen fathers also tend to perceive more conflict in their relationships than older fathers (Nakashima & Camp 1984) (see chapter 4).

Antecedent Data

There are serious difficulties in the use of antecedent data that were collected on teenagers *before* they became fathers (for example, Card & Wise 1978; Pauker 1971; Russ-Eft, Sprenger & Beever 1979). These studies usually contain large data pools that are reanalyzed several years after data collection (sometimes as long as twenty-five years later) and that use variables that were not originally intended for study. Antecedent data have been used on teen fathers to eliminate certain biases that show up when males are studied *after* the unfortunate out-of-wedlock experience. For instance, studies on teen fathers after their knowledge of the pregnancy catch them at a time of depression and emotional conflict and lead to the conclusion that teen fathers are psychologically worse off than their nonfather contemporaries (Pannor & Evans 1967).

In addressing this issue, Pauker (1971) argued that many reports of psychological maladjustment among teenage fathers occur because data are assessed *after* the traumatic out-of-wedlock experience, in which stress and emotional conflicts had surfaced. To prove his point, Pauker studied MMPI, ACE Psychological and Cooperative English Test scores of ninety-four Minnesota boys, aged 13 to 19 *before* they had fathered a child. In addition, ninety-four control boys were selected who attended the same school, were of similar age, and were from similar socioeconomic backgrounds, but who had not fathered a child. Overall, teen fathers were psychologically and intellectually more alike than different from the matched group of nonfathers.

Although researchers employing antecedent data are to be applauded for their efforts to overcome biased outcomes, a shortcoming of another kind emerges with this approach. Antecedent data obtained from these large survey pools are often reanalyzed many years later. Card and Wise (1978), for instance, used a data base from Project Talent generated in 1960. Eighteen years later, they analyzed these responses obtained from a nationwide random sample of 375,000 boys and girls from 1,225 senior and junior high schools. The survey examined the subjects at one, five, and eleven years after high school. Teenage parents included respondents who became parents before their twentieth birthday. Given the nature of the substantive social, economic, and cultural shifts which have occurred between the date of sampling and analysis, crucial questions arise in terms of relevance and generalizability to contemporary society. It is possible, for example, that epidemic proportions of adolescent parenthood during the intervening years between 1960 and 1987 have changed the nature of how this phenomenon is perceived by society and consequently how the experience affects the teenage father.

Also drawing from the Project Talent data pool, Russ-Eft, Sprenger, and Beever (1979) brought the issue of adolescent parenting into contemporary focus by examining both the *antecedents* and *consequences* of early childbearing. In contrast to the Card and Wise study, Russ-Eft followed up the antecedent data with in-depth interviews of 500 men and 500 women who had participated in Project Talent and were teenage parents.

Although it is informative to place the psychological experience of teenage fatherhood in a contemporary demographic context, Earls and Siegel (1980) underscore the need for distinguishing modern-day youth from their earlier counterparts due to an increasing emphasis on personal liberty in self-expression and human relations:

> Images promoting "free expression" of sexuality are pervasively represented in contemporary society, and it is against this background that changes in the orientation of young people toward sexual activity are taking place. Cultural trends are supported by the fact that adolescents are experimenting with sexuality at an earlier age than ever. (p. 473)

Adolescent Males

Another trend leading to inferential data is the assessment of contraceptive knowledge and use as well as attitudes toward pregnancy of adolescent males who are not necessarily teenage fathers (for example, Clark, Zabin & Hardy 1984; Finkel & Finkel 1975, 1978; Johnson & Staples 1979; Redmond 1985, Vadies & Hale 1979). These data are frequently generalized to include all teenage males, including teen fathers, despite the fact that research indicates important differences between teen fathers and nonfathers in their views toward contraceptive practices and adolescent pregnancy (Robbins & Lynn 1973; Rivara, Sweeney & Henderson 1985). Some studies, containing mixed samples of adolescent fathers and adolescent nonfathers, fail to analyze possible differences between the two groups. Moreover, studies—such as Redmond (1985)—present hypothetical situations to which teenage males may respond one way although their actual behaviors may indicate the contrary.

Direct Sources of Information

Exclusive of the four inferential sources of research data and two small anecdotal accounts (Carparulo & London 1981, Herzog 1984), an extensive review of the literature identifies only twenty-one studies from 1973 to 1987 that directly sample a population of adolescent fathers (see table 5–1). Although an improvement over inferential sources, these studies are rife with problems. Three studies (Brown 1983, de Lissovoy 1973a, 1973b) assessed the adolescent-couple relationship, whereas the remainder exclusively studied teenage fathers and, with one exception, did not use marital status of the adolescent fathers as a variable for study (Fry & Trifiletti 1983).

Slightly more than half of these studies (52 percent) are descriptive in the sense that they employ small samples of adolescent fathers and have no comparison groups. The remaining 48 percent of the studies compare teenage fathers with their nonfather agemates (29 percent), compare teenage fathers with adult fathers (14 percent), or compare married teenage fathers with unmarried teenage fathers (5 percent). As table 5–1 indicates, all sample sizes are small, age ranges vary widely, and nonrandomized designs are routinely employed. The majority of the research in this area (95 percent of the studies) is based on self-report data such as interviews (62 percent) or self-administered questionnaires (33 percent). Only one investigation has used a behavioral measure (5 percent).

Unrepresentative Sampling

Studies employing inferential research sources are important historically because they built a knowledge base about adolescent parents and generated scientific interest and concern over the teenage father issue. In one of the few national studies on adolescent male sexuality (Sorenson 1973), problems emerged. Although it included more than 400 male and female teenagers, the sample did not represent the national population because many subjects were withdrawn due to parental objections.

Even as direct adolescent father samples became commonplace, some anecdotal reports did more to reinforce the stereotype than to represent an accurate picture. For instance, Herzog's (1984) clinical sample of six white, middle-class teenage boys was depicted as cavalier towards adolescent pregnancy. The three case studies presented by Caparulo and London (1981)

Table 5–1
Demographic and Methodological Characteristics of Studies Directly Assessing Teenage Fathers

Study	Age	SES	Race	Sample Size	Locale	Method	Design
Descriptive/ Noncomparative Studies							
de Lissovoy (1973a)	M=17	Low	White (100%)	48	Rural Northeast	Interview/ Questionn	Conven
de Lissovoy (1973b)	M=17	Low	White (100%)	37	Rural Northeast	Interview/ Questionn	Conven
Hendricks (1980)	<21	Low	Black (100%)	20	Urban Southwest	Interview	"
Elster & Panzarine (1980)	M=17.4	Low	Black (62%)	16	Urban Southeast	Interview/ Questionn	"
Hendricks (1983)	<21	Low	Black (100%)	95	Urban West/ Midwest	Interview	"
Barret & Robinson (1982)	M=18.7	Low	Black (85%)	26	Urban South	Questionn	"
Brown (1983)	R=16–21	Low	Black (100%)	33	Urban North	Interview	"
Elster & Panzarine (1983)	M=17.6	Middle	White (90%)	20	Urban West	Interview	"
Panzarine & Elster (1983)	M=17.6	Middle	White (90%)	20	Urban West	Interview	"
Vaz, Smolen & Miller (1983)	M=18.9	Low	Black (100%)	41	Urban South	Interview	"
Westney, Cole & Munford (1986)	M=17.4	UKN	UKN	28	Urban Northeast	Questionn	"

(*cont.*)

Table 5–1. continued

Study	Age	SES	Race	Sample Size	Locale	Method	Design
Studies Comparing Teen Fathers and Teen Nonfathers							
Robbins & Lynn (1973)	M=17.11	Middle/ Low	White (59%)	22	Urban West	Interview	"
Robinson, Barret & Skeen (1983)	M=17.5	Low	Black (85%)	20	Urban South	Questionn	"
McCoy & Tyler (1985)	R=15–19	Low	Black (100%)	24	Urban Northeast	Questionn	"
Redmond (1985)	M=18.5	UKN	UKN	74	Canada	Questionn	"
Rivara, Sweeney & Henderson (1985)	M=17.5	Low	Black (100%)	100	Urban South	Interview	"
Rivara, Sweeney & Henderson (1986)	M=19	Low	Black (100%)	81	Urban South	Interview	"
Studies Comparing Teen Fathers and Adult Fathers							
Nakashima & Camp (1984)	M=17.9	UKN	UKN	20	Urban West	Questionn	"
Lamb & Elster (1985)	M=16.5	Low/ Middle	White (86%)	18	Urban West	Questionn/ Naturalistic Observation	"
Robinson & Barret (1987)	M=16.9	Low	Black (100%)	12	Urban South	Questionn	"
Studies Comparing Married Teen Fathers and Unwed Teen Fathers							
Fry & Trifiletti (1983)	R=17.5–18.6	Low	White (100%)	95	Suburban	Interview	"

Note: M = mean, UKN = unknown, R = range.

equally portrayed the young fathers as uncaring, immature, and irresponsible. The authors even made tentative conclusions based on three interviews that contributed to old biases: "One of the stereotypes of teenage fathers—as persons without feelings for either their offspring or the teenage mother—seems thus partially true and partially false." (p. 32).

More systematic research has relied solely on convenience or matched samples. As table 5–1 shows, a random study of teen fathers has not been possible. The information we have directly from teenage fathers is based predominantly on self-report data, namely self-administered questionnaires and face-to-face interviews with young males who are willing to participate. Both of these approaches, though useful, have certain built-in biases. Teenage fathers who are unknown or who have withdrawn all contact and support from the mothers are omitted from study. In addition, as Belsky and Miller (1986) point out, adolescent mothers are the gatekeepers through which adolescent fathers are (or are not) identified; and adolescent mothers have many motives and pressures in making this decision.

Young men who choose to participate in research may give responses that they think will please the interviewer or that will make them look good on paper. In addition, the investigator cannot be certain that respondents actually behave in accordance with what is reported. Lack of consistency between self-report data and actual behaviors is well documented in many areas of research. Another drawback is that respondents must be able to read and write in order to participate in pen and paper studies. Many subjects participating in teenage father research are unskilled at reading and writing, and questions on written assessments sometimes require a sophistication of literate skills. Subjects have been limited to predominantly black, urban, low-income males whose ages range from 14.5 to 24. Sample sizes are small, ranging from 6 to 100.

Historically, fewer young unmarried fathers, compared to mothers, have maintained contact with human service agencies, hospitals, and health clinics which, through their work in this area, provide most of the data pools. Conducting studies with adolescent males has been difficult because these young men are generally reluctant to come forward and the agencies that routinely interact with them often cite confidentiality reasons for not supporting well-planned research activities.

But as adolescent male populations become more accessible through nationwide programs designed exclusively for teen fathers and increases in school-based health clinics (see chapter 8), reliance on unrepresentative samples will no longer suffice. In the next several years, as the need for more information is realized and agencies aggressively begin to make available more services to teenage fathers, more adolescent males will benefit from services. As this happens, national data, utilizing randomized designs, will not only be possible but essential.

The implications of this analysis are clear. The profile we use to understand and describe adolescent fathers is far from conclusive. Clearly, the literature has advanced with an increase, after 1983, in the utilization of comparison groups with teenage fathers as well as less emphasis on self-report questionnaires and more on interview data and the beginnings of behavioral measures. Still, until researchers can obtain larger, more representative samples that employ more sophisticated research designs, caution should be exercised in making sweeping generalizations about adolescent fathers. Meanwhile, it is possible to make only limited speculations from some indirect sources and from a handful of direct sources that pave the way for future inquiry.

Suggestions for Future Research

The sampling and methodological flaws previously discussed have gone largely overlooked due to a need for creating a data base. However, sampling and methodological specificity will become increasingly important as more researchers begin to address this field of study. A number of actions can be taken that will improve the quality of research on the teenage father and ultimately our understanding of him.

Additional Research

An increase in the sheer quantity of studies on adolescent pregnancy that either include teen fathers or focus on them exclusively. Direct sources of research assessment should be used, with adolescent mothers never used as voices for teen fathers. Little is known about the paternal grandparents' role in childrearing and teenage pregnancy. More research is needed in this area (Allen-Meares 1984).

Cooperation from the Helping Professions

Helping professionals can cooperate, within legal and ethical confidentiality constraints, with researchers of adolescent pregnancy. Funding agencies, social agencies, and researchers can combine their resources to improve the information base about young fathers. Funding agencies can also be more sensitive to the many obstacles that researchers encounter in attempting to gather meaningful information.

Health clinics, hospitals, and other human services agencies that routinely deal with unwed pregnancy and adoption can cooperate with research efforts and begin to request interviews with fathers as a routine part of their services. Social agencies also can be more cooperative with researchers by coordinating group meetings of teenage mothers with fathers where data could be gathered. Schools, which deal with many of the results of adolescent pregnancy, could invite researchers to make presentations to student groups that probably include these young fathers. Although it is important for agencies to protect their clients from exploitation by researchers, well-developed research activities conducted by ethical professionals will ultimately improve the nature and quality of services rendered.

Representative Samples

Because adolescent fathers are difficult to reach, research on them is more expensive and time-consuming than similar research on teenage mothers. Still, with increasing awareness and inclusion of teenage fathers in social programs, researchers can lead the way by well-planned studies that include representative samples and that avoid confounding variables. Although these young men are often reluctant to identify themselves, it is believed that more of them will step forward once individuals and agencies in the helping professions begin to respond to their needs. A word of caution with this approach, however, is in order, as Lerman (1986) points out: "Data based on young fathers entering a program or based on referrals from unmarried mothers are unlikely to be representative of all young fathers." (p. 6). To control for this factor, a national study with randomly selected teen fathers has been suggested by a number of experts (Barret and Robinson 1985, Earls & Siegel 1980). Although in the past a truly representative sample was rarely obtained, with the proper funds, researchers could develop a network that links many of the innovative programs that exist across the country.

Age as a Critical Variable

There is no consensus among researchers on the ages that should be used to define teenage fathers. Age ranges are unclear and inconsistent from one study to the next. Although 17-year-old teen fathers (see table 5–1) seem to be the most commonly studied, many researchers lump together different ages, which range from 14.5 to 24 years. Rothstein (1978), for example, in his study of adolescent males, fatherhood, and abortion, defined his adolescent subjects as 24 years of age or younger. Selected age ranges from other studies were 14.5 to 19 (de Lissovoy 1973a, 1973b), 16 to 21 (Barret & Robinson 1982, Robbins & Lynn 1973), 17 to 18 (Elster & Panzarine 1983), and 15 to 19 (McCoy & Tyler 1985).

When studies group teenagers with older men or lump adolescent fathers with unmarried men, the developmental variable of premature fatherhood is confounded. Sixteen-year-olds are very different from 21-year-olds and thus the relevance of these studies to all teen fathers is questionable.

Some scholars even question the common practice of lumping all teenagers together in one category (Harrison 1982). They point out that the term
teenager is far too broad a category to use for research purposes and that 13-
year-olds in junior high school have different biological and social-emotional
needs and problems from 19-year-olds who have completed secondary
schooling and have perhaps married. They recommend the subdivisions of
school age and those who are out of school. The consensus was that age
should be used only as one identifying factor in future research.

Deficiencies in Reporting Demographic Variables

Several studies failed to report certain demographic information—such as
socioeconomic status and race—that must be known before useful generalizations of all teenage fathers can be drawn. We know, for example, that var-
iability exists in adolescent male sexuality among different ethnic groups, as
when black and Hispanic youth become sexually active earlier and are less
likely to use contraception (Finkel & Finkel 1975). Elster and Lamb (1986)
also note that more refined categories than "under 20 years of age" should
be provided in reporting age characteristics. Another problem is illustrated
by a study that, while providing the first behavioral measure on teen fathers,
confounds the variable of fatherhood. The male partners used by Lamb and
Elster (1985), for instance, included five subjects who were not biological
fathers of the infants. The degree to which this variable confuses the findings
is unclear. Future data sets should provide as much detail and consistency as
possible regarding demographics of the samples.

New Nomenclature

Development of a new and more positive nomenclature in the area of adolescent pregnancies is needed. Teenage fathers are frequently called "putative
fathers," "alleged fathers," "boyfriends," or even "precocious fathers." Terms
such a these hardly attract young men and do little to help society's negative
image of these young men. There are also no terms to describe the adolescent
mother-father relationship. They may still be boyfriend-girlfriend, but clearly
once a child is produced, a more serious relationship has evolved. Constant
references to "the mother of your baby" seem awkward.

Relevant Comparison Groups

Rather than investigating samples of teenage fathers for descriptive and non-
comparative purposes, designs should contain relevant comparison groups to
advance what we already know in this area. For example, more information

is needed on possible social and psychological differences between teenage fathers and their nonfather contemporaries, teenage fathers and older adult fathers, and married teenage fathers and unmarried teenage fathers.

Research questions might include the following: Are there differences between teen fathers who never marry the mother and those who do? Are there differences between young men who are intensely involved in the fathering experience and those who remain aloof? In what ways are teen fathers different from or similar to adult men who father children by adolescent females and adult men who father children by adult women? How do teen fathers actually interact with their infants compared to males in these other comparison groups? What factors differentially influence the parenting practices of males in these comparison groups? What is the social and psychological aftermath experienced by older adult men who, after fathering children as teenagers, lose contact with mother and baby? (Chapter 6 presents some preliminary efforts in this regard.)

Longitudinal Studies

Long-term studies are needed to follow teenage fathers over time to assess attitudinal and behavioral differences in fathering and family life from adolescence to adulthood. Future longitudinal investigations should also address the kinds of long-term adjustments and adaptions that are made or need to be made by teenage fathers (Fry & Trifiletti 1983). The transition to fatherhood as well as effects on children can be monitored at different age levels. Those subjects who are first-time fathers in adolescence and second-time fathers in adulthood can be studied for developmental differences. Those subjects who are fathers in adolescence and lose contact with mother and baby can be studied as adult men to measure potential psychological aftereffects.

Data Collection

A multimethod approach to data collection in which observational techniques are used in conjunction with the traditional self-report and interview techniques will yield more sophisticated data and lead to a better understanding of teenage fathers. This approach will also enable study of actual behaviors rather than reliance on perceptions. Only one study has employed this approach in its investigation of adolescent fathers (Lamb & Elster 1985).

It is essential that future research employ a systems-oriented approach and assess perceptions and behaviors of adolescent mothers and fathers, as well as those of the grandparents, with the baby. Maintaining an ecological focus is crucial as teenage fathers are observed interacting in their natural environments—not in the researcher's laboratory. Researchers need multivariate designs with large samples that will provide data on the interaction of significant variables that impact on adolescent mothers and fathers.

References

Allen-Meares, P. (1984) Adolescent pregnancy and parenting: The forgotten adolescent father and his parents. *Journal of Social Work and Human Sexuality* 3:27–38.

Babikian, H.M., & Goldman, A. (1971) A study of teenage pregnancy. *American Journal of Psychiatry* 128:755–60.

Barret, R.L., & Robinson, B.E. (1981) Teenage fathers: A profile. *Personnel and Guidance Journal* 60:226–28.

———. (1982) A descriptive study of teenage expectant fathers. *Family Relations* 31:349–52.

———. (1985) "The adolescent father." In S. Hanson & F. Bozett (eds.), *Dimensions of fatherhood.* Beverly Hills, Ca.: Sage.

———. (1986) Adolescent fathers: Often forgotten parents. *Pediatric Nursing* 12:273–77.

———. (1987) "Adolescent fatherhood: Correlates and consequences." In A.R. Stiffman & R.A. Feldman (eds.), *Advances in adolescent mental health. Vol. IV, Sexual activity, childbearing and childrearing.* Greenwich, Conn.: JAI Press.

Belsky, J., & Miller, B.C. (1986) "Adolescent fatherhood in the context of the transition to parenthood." In A. Elster & M. Lamb (eds.), *Adolescent fatherhood,* pp. 107–22. Hillsdale, New Jersey: Lawrence Erlbaum.

Brown, S.V. (1983) The commitment and concerns of black adolescent parents. *Social Work Research & Abstracts* 19:27–34.

Card, J.J., & Wise, L.L. (1978) Teenage mothers and teenage fathers: The impact of early childbearing on the parents' personal and professional lives. *Family Planning Perspectives* 10:199–205.

Caparulo, F., & London, K. (1981) Adolescent fathers: Adolescents first, fathers second. *Issues in Health Care of Women* 3:23–33.

Chilman, C. (1979) *Adolescent sexuality in a changing American society.* Washington, D.C.: National Institutes of Health.

Clark, S.D., Zabin, L.S., & Hardy, J.B. (1984) Sex, contraception, and parenthood: Experience and attitudes among urban black youth. *Family Planning Perspectives* 16:77–82.

Connolly, L. (1978) Boy fathers. *Human Behavior* (January):40–43.

de Lissovoy, V. (1973a) Child care by adolescent parents. *Children Today* 2:22–25.

———. (1973b) High school marriages: A longitudinal study. *Journal of Marriage and the Family* 35:245–55.

Earls, F., & Siegel, B. (1980) Precocious fathers. *American Journal of Orthopsychiatry* 50:469–80.

Elster, A.B., & Lamb, M.E. (1986) *Adolescent fatherhood.* Hillsdale, New Jersey: Lawrence Erlbaum.

Elster, A.B., & Panzarine, S. (1980) Unwed teenage fathers: Emotional and health educational needs. *Journal of Adolescent Health Care* 1:116–20.

———. (1983) Teenage fathers: Stresses during gestation and early parenthood. *Clinical Pediatrics* 22:700–703.

Finkel, M., & Finkel, D. (1975) Sexual and contraceptive knowledge, attitudes and behavior of male adolescents. *Family Planning Perspectives* 7:256–60.

———. (1978) Male adolescent contraceptive utilization. *Adolescence* 13:443–51.

Fry, P.S., & Trifiletti, R.J. (1983) Teenage fathers: An exploration of their developmental needs and anxieties and the implications for clinical-social intervention and services. *Journal of Psychiatric Treatment & Evaluation* 5:219–27.

Furstenberg, F.F. (1976) *Unplanned parenthood: The social consequences of teenage childbearing*. New York: The Free Press.

Furstenberg, F.F., & Talvitie, K.G. (1980) Children's names and paternal claims: Bonds between unmarried fathers and their children. *Journal of Family Issues* 1:31–57.

Gershenson, H.P. (1983) Redefining fatherhood in families with white adolescent mothers. *Journal of Marriage and the Family* 45:591–99.

Hanson, S., & Bozett, F. (1985) *Dimensions of fatherhood*. Beverly Hills, Ca.: Sage.

Harrison, C.E. (1982) "Teenage pregnancy." In D.L. Parron & L. Eisenberg (eds.), *Infants at risk for developmental dysfunction,* pp. 43–55. Washington, D.C.: National Academy Press.

Hendricks, L.E. (1980) Unwed adolescent fathers: Problems they face and their sources of social support. *Adolescence* 15:862–69.

———. (1983) Suggestions for reaching unmarried black adolescent fathers. *Child Welfare* 62:141–46.

Hendricks, L.E., Howard, C.S., & Caesar, P.P. (1981a) Black unwed adolescent fathers: A comparative study of their problems and help-seeking behavior. *Journal of the National Medical Association* 73:863–68.

———. (1981b) Help-seeking behavior among select populations of black unmarried adolescent fathers: Implications for human service agencies. *American Journal of Public Health* 7:733–35.

Herzog, J.M. (1984) "Boys who make babies." In M. Sugar (ed.), *Adolescent parenthood*. New York: Spectrum Publications.

Johnson, L.B., & Staples, R.E. (1979) Family planning and the young minority male: A pilot project. *The Family Coordinator* 28:535–43.

Lamb, M. (1979) Paternal influences and the father's role: A personal perspective. *The American Psychologist* 34:938–43.

Lamb, M., & Elster, A.B. (1985) Adolescent mother-infant-father relationships. *Developmental Psychology* 21:768–73.

Leashore, B.R. (1979) Human services and the unmarried father: The forgotten half. *The Family Coordinator* 28:529–34.

LeMasters, E.E., & DeFrain, J. (1983) *Parents in contemporary America: A sympathetic view*. Homewood, Illinois: Dorsey.

Lerman, R.I. (1986) Who are the young absent fathers? *Youth and Society* 18:3–27.

Lorenzi, M.E., Klerman, L.V., & Jekel, J.F. (1977) School-age parents: How permanent a relationship? *Adolescence* 12:13–22.

McCoy, J.E., & Tyler, F.B. (1985) Selected psychosocial characteristics of black un-wed adolescent fathers. *Journal of Adolescent Health Care* 6:12–16.

Mueller, J. (1970) Reconciliation or resignation: A case study. *The Family Coordinator* 19:345–52.

Nakashima, I.I., & Camp, B.W. (1984) Fathers of infants born to adolescent mothers. *American Journal of Diseases of Children* 138:452–54.

Pannor, R., & Evans, B.W. (1967) The unmarried father: An integral part of casework services to the unmarried mother. *Child Welfare* 44:16–20.

Pannor, R., Massarik, F., & Evans, B. (1971) *The unmarried father: New approaches for helping unmarried young parents.* New York: Springer.

Panzarine, S.A., & Elster, A.B. (1983) Coping in a group of expectant adolescent fathers: An exploratory study. *Journal of Adolescent Health Care* 4:117–20.

Pauker, J.D. (1971) Fathers of children conceived out of wedlock: Pregnancy, high school, psychological test results. *Developmental Psychology* 4:215–18.

Pfuhl, E.H. (1978) The unwed father: A non-deviant rule breaker. *Sociological Quarterly* 19:113–28.

Platts, H.K. (1968) A public adoption agency's approach to natural fathers. *Child Welfare* 47:530–37.

Redmond, M.A. (1985) Attitudes of adolescent males toward adolescent pregnancy and fatherhood. *Family Relations* 34:337–42.

Rivara, F.P., Sweeney, P.J., & Henderson, B.F. (1985) A study of low socioeconomic status black teenage fathers and their nonfather peers. *Pediatrics* 75:648–56.

———. (1986) Black teenage fathers: What happens when the child is born? *Pediatrics* 78:151–58.

Robbins, M.M., & Lynn, D. (1973) The unwed fathers: Generation, recidivism and attitudes about intercourse in California Youth Authority wards. *Journal of Sex Research* 9:334–41.

Robinson, B.E., & Barret, R.L. (1982) Issues and problems related to the research of teenage fathers: A critical analysis. *Journal of School Health* 52:596–600.

———. (1986) *The developing father.* New York: The Guilford Press.

———. (1987) Self-concept and anxiety of adolescent and adult fathers. *Adolescence.* In press.

Robinson, B.E., Barret, R.L., & Skeen, P. (1983) Locus of control of unwed adolescent fathers versus adolescent nonfathers. *Perceptual and Motor Skills* 56:397–98.

Rothstein, A.A. (1978) Adolescent males, fatherhood, and abortion. *Journal of Youth and Adolescence* 7:203–14.

Russ-Eft, D., Sprenger, M., & Beever, H. (1979) Antecedents of adolescent parenthood and consequences at age 30. *The Family Coordinator* 28:173–79.

Safilios-Rothschild, C. (1969) Family sociology or wives' family sociology? A cross-cultural examination on decision-making. *Journal of Marriage and the Family* 31:290–301.

Scott, K., Field, T., & Robertson, E. (eds.) (1980) *Teenage parents and their offspring.* New York: Grune & Stratton.

Seeley, J.R. (1956) *Crestwood Heights.* New York: Basic Books.

Sorenson, R. (1973) *Adolescent sexuality in contemporary America.* New York: World Publishing Company.

Vadies, E., & Hale, D. (1979) Adolescent males: Attitudes toward abortion, contraception, and sexuality. *Advances in Planned Parenthood* 13:35–41.

Vaz, R., Smolen, P., & Miller, C. (1983) Adolescent pregnancy: Involvement of the male partner. *Journal of Adolescent Health Care.* 4:246–50.

Vincent, C. (1960) Unmarried fathers and the mores: "Sexual exploiter" as an ex post facto label. *American Sociological Review* 25:40–46.

Westney, O.E., Cole, J., & Munford, T.L. (1986) Adolescent unwed prospective fathers: Readiness for fatherhood and behaviors toward the mother and the expected infant. *Adolescence* 21:901–11.

Zelnik, M., & Kantner, J. (1972) "Sexuality, contraception and pregnancy among young unwed females in the United States." In C.F. Westoff and R. Parke (eds.), *Demographic and social aspects of population growth and American future research report.* Washington, D.C.: U.S. Government Printing Office.

———. (1979) Reasons for nonuse of contraceptives by sexually active women, ages 15–19. *Family Planning Perspectives* 11:289–94.

6
Teenage Fatherhood Revisited: Adult Men Recall Their Experiences

Robert L. Barret
University of North Carolina at Charlotte

At age 33, Mike looks back on his adolescence as a time of challenge. A father at 16, it would have been easy for him to drop out of school and stick with the job of washing cars at his father's business. But something made him stay in school and try to balance the demands of being a young father and husband and provider while holding on to his goal of becoming a pilot. No longer married to the mother of his 17-year-old son, today he has realized much success. He lives in a fine house and flies for a major airline. He knows that the cost of his success was great in terms of his marriage and his relationship with his son, but mostly he felt that he was doing what he "had" to do.

By age 15, Mike and his girlfriend had been having sex regularly, and Mike thought that was pretty neat. He liked her a lot even though somehow he knew that he would not want to spend the rest of his life with her. They didn't use birth control because, "I always pulled out just before I came," and they didn't worry too much about her getting pregnant. That wasn't even talked about much; mostly they were just kids having a good time with each other and their friends. When the doctor confirmed she was pregnant both of them panicked. Abortion was not as acceptable in 1970 as it is today and really wasn't seen as an alternative. Mike knew that he would marry her even though he did so with a sinking feeling, knowing that his dream of the Air Force Academy was over. They visited with the minister of his church, who became a major source of support for Mike. Their parents arranged a quiet wedding, and they moved in with her family. He quit the football team and took two jobs after school.

Things were rough at first. His in-laws' house was small, and they had very little privacy; because of his work they had little time together other than the moments squeezed in between his obligations. Moving to his parents' home was not much better, and soon they decided to get their own place in a public housing project. That was the best time for them. He was so focused on providing for his family that he never really missed his friends. His teachers made allowances for him, recognizing that he was overloaded. Others in the community also rallied behind them. Mike's attitude was, "I created this situation, and it's my responsibility to take care of my wife and son." He did not resent what he had given up, mostly because, *"I hardly had time to think about anything other than trying to stay awake in school and do well on my jobs."*

The marriage ended in divorce two years after high school. Mike worked his way through college, seeing his son as often as possible but still determined to learn to fly. He worked odd jobs around a small airport in return for flying lessons. He remembers leaving his son at the airport with a box of toys while he gained air time flying sky divers on weekends. Later he was hired by a private company to fly executives around the country. Many weekends he would meet his son, Hank, at the bus and have to face his tears as he told him that he had to go back to his mother since he had been called to fly to a distant city and would be gone for days.

But once he got a more secure job and remarried he began to develop a more predictable relationship with his son. Now even though they live in different cities, Mike talks with Hank regularly and becomes a full-time father in the summer when Hank comes to live with him. It is obvious that there is a lot of love between them and that they have put those early years behind them.

Teenage fathers are emerging as young men who frequently want to be quite active as fathers. Earlier in this book you read about some of them who participate in their children's lives in many different ways. When given the chance, teenage fathers are involved in raising their children; they often have daily contact, contribute money, and participate in decisions regarding their welfare (Barret & Robinson 1982, Robinson & Barret 1986). It is also true that research on teenage fathers is flawed by the unavailability of representative sampling, but we are learning that the stereotype of the teenage father as an uncaring and uninvolved male is not always true and that when given the chance many of them report that the fathering experience is a central event in their young lives (Barret & Robinson 1987, Robinson & Barret 1982, 1987).

Herzog (1984) has suggested that boys raise their self-esteem by becoming teenage fathers and that the nature of the relationship to their girlfriends is the most important factor in the fathering response. Other factors that have influenced the father's involvement with fathering include federal, state, and local welfare assistance policies (Vinkousis 1986), the duration of the relationship, its exclusivity and level of commitment, the discussion of a possible pregnancy and the subsequent use of birth control, and the male's relationships with his friends (Belsky & Miller 1986). These factors will be used to examine the cases that appear in the following to see how they influenced the fathering experience.

But how do teen dads view fatherhood years later in adulthood? What is the impact of such early fathering on their teenage years? Do they maintain contact for more than a few years and do they ever become custodial parents on a full-time basis? In retrospect, how do they assess the influence of early fathering on their adult lives? How are the predictors made by professionals, such as those mentioned in the preceding paragraph, evaluated in light of the fathers' lives? The purpose of this chapter is to provide some insight into questions such as these. But before addressing these questions, I will detail the procedures I used to find these fathers and a profile of their characteristics.

Case Study Procedures

Unfortunately, the professional literature does not include data drawn from adults who struggled with fatherhood during their teenage years. So, in order to gather information for this chapter I searched out some men over the age of 25 who had been teenage fathers and interviewed them about the impact of early parenthood on their adult lives. Finding these men was a difficult task, and admittedly, this is probably a very biased sample because it consists of men who were willing to come forward because they have something they want others to understand. There is also a possibility that they have responded to questions in socially desirable ways that present their fathering experiences in a more positive light. Conclusions must be carefully drawn with an awareness that this small sample is not representative of all teenage fathers. The information gained from them must be seen as preliminary data that provide isolated glimpses into the lives of men who were teenage fathers. At the same time, given the paucity of information drawn from adults who were teenage fathers, these data are useful.

Much of the research on teenage fathers reveals the difficulties in obtaining subjects (Robinson & Barret 1982). But if teenage fathers are hard to find, locating men who were teenage fathers is even harder. Efforts to reach men over the age of 25 who had fathered children while teenagers included placing advertisements in newspapers, making public announcements, and contacting agencies such as probation offices, the Salvation Army, medical facilities, church groups, student groups, and so on. Whereas many teenage fathers can be found in predictable places such as schools, teenage pregnancy clinics, and recreation centers, in later years they tend to disappear into many different areas, and often they may not want to dredge up feelings related to events that are in their past.

Through the means described, a small group of ten men came forward and agreed to be interviewed about their fathering experience. Table 6–1 presents an overview of some of the characteristics of these men.

Table 6–1
Profile of Subjects on Related Variables

	Black	*White*	*Total*
Mean age	27	36.6	31.8
Mean education (years)	13.2	15.2	14.2
Est. income (thousands)	13.6	27.2	20.4
Used birth control			
Yes	1	3	4
No	4	2	6
Present at Birth			
Yes	2	5	7
No	3	0	3

Profile of Case Study Subjects

The men who participated in this study came from a variety of backgrounds and have achieved various levels of success in their adult lives. The material in this chapter is drawn from structured interviews conducted with these men, five black, five white, whose ages range from 22 to 40. Two of them remain in the relationships that created the unplanned adolescent pregnancy. Four are divorced but still involved as fathers, and four never married their pregnant girlfriends but have varying degrees of connections with their children. These men work in positions that include sales, marketing, hospital orderly, airline pilot, auto parts house manager, school custodian, clergyman, construction worker, and shop clerk.

The following brief descriptions give names and specifics about each of the fathers. Although pseudonyms are used to protect their identities, the general facts of their real-life experiences are reported as they were told to me. Four of these fathers were chosen for thorough case analysis and will be discussed in detail later in the chapter.

Thomas

A 27-year-old worker in a food processing plant, Thomas became a teenage father at age 16. The experience appears to have had little outward impact on his life. He lost contact with his girlfriend and never saw the baby. Today he lives with the mother of his 2-year-old daughter.

Mike

An airline pilot, Mike is featured in the beginning of this chapter. He married his pregnant girlfriend when he was 16 years old and finished high school and college. Although the marriage did not last, he continues to be a constant factor in his son's life. Today he has been remarried for eight years, and he and his wife have no children.

Richard

Married at age 18, Richard is discussed in more detail later in the chapter. His son was born during his freshman year at college. A person of great energy, Richard finished college, worked for a few years, entered seminary, and became a minister in an inner-city neighborhood. Currently divorced, Richard recently allowed his 17-year-old son to return home following his expulsion from school for alcohol and drug abuse difficulties. His daughter lives with his ex-wife.

James

Following the birth of his son when he was 15, James and his girlfriend began to live together so their son would have a better chance in life than they had. Nine years later they are still together, and James has finished college and is beginning his career as a leader in a group home for troubled teenagers. He and his girlfriend do not have other children.

Marcus

Now 26 years old, Marcus works in construction. His daughter, whom he has never seen, was born when he was 15. Today Marcus talks about that experience sadly. "I kept trying to help out, but she just told me to stay away. Her parents wouldn't let me talk to her, and my mother said it would be best if I just forgot about her. I asked my mom to help, but she said she'd done the same thing to her boyfriend when I was born. After my daughter was born, I went by a couple of times, but they treated me like I was the devil and wouldn't let me in. After a while I quit trying and today I don't even know where she is." Marcus is now married and has one child.

Jerome

Twenty-six-year-old Jerome works in a hospital as an orderly. His son was born when he was 16, and for a while he saw him regularly. "I used to take money to his mother and play with him whenever I could." But after a few months the relationship between Jerome and his girlfriend got bad because he was going out with someone else. "She told me that if I wouldn't quit going out with other women, she would take my baby away and I'd never see my son again. One day I came around to see the baby and she was gone! Her family still won't tell me where she went. Every now and then I take some money by their house and ask them to give it to him, but they still don't want me to see him." Jerome is not married and has fathered two other children.

Danny

At 38, Danny is a manager of an auto parts house. His son was born when he was 19, which gave him an excuse to drop out of school. "I was never a good student anyway; unfortunately he has turned out a lot like me in that respect. Recently he dropped out of high school." Danny and his girlfriend had married before their son was born. Initially the pregnancy was a shock even though they had not been using birth control. He took her to the doctor and neither of them ever talked about abortion. The early years were rough as he jumped into the provider role while trying to learn what it meant to be a husband and a father at the same time. The marriage lasted thirteen years, and today Danny has remarried and until recently has had his son living with him. He and his present wife have no children.

Allan

The oldest of the fathers, Allan is 40 and enjoys his relationship with his daughter, who is now 23. But that has not always been the case. He and his ex-wife learned of the pregnancy during his freshman year of college. The first couple of years of their marriage were good times for all of them, mostly because they had the emotional and financial backing of their families. After the marriage dissolved, Allan continued in school and went on to earn a doctorate in history. His daughter visited during the summer and at Christmas but gradually he lost touch with her. "Her mother remarried three times and Cory took the name of one of those men. After a while I was a stranger to her, and sometimes I resented having to send the support money. But in the past few years we have gotten close and now we really have fun together. I've taken her to Europe with me and enjoy seeing her be so successful." Allan is currently divorced from his second wife with whom he had a son.

Kenneth

Thirty-six-year-old Kenneth has two children who were born during his teenage years. He sees them almost every day even though their mother and grandmother do not encourage his coming around. "I know they will never really let me be the father I want to be. But I figure that since I give them money, I can come to visit." Kenneth now works as a school custodian; he is married and has one child.

Hank

Still married to his high school girlfriend, 36-year-old Hank has two children: a daughter, who was born while he was in the twelfth grade, and a son, born three years later. Although there have been lots of good times in the past seventeen years, the marriage has not been a happy one. Supported by family and friends, it has been difficult to decide what to do. "Sometimes I think we would all be happier if I just left. But it's hard to just walk out on my kids. I want them to know that I love them and that I am here for them."

Case Examples and Discussion

James: Using Fatherhood to Escape from Welfare

James became involved with Denice when he was 14 and she was 18. During the early months of their relationship they became sexually active. James, the youngest of nine children, had told her that he did not want her to get pregnant and that it was up to her to use birth control. He did not want to have a child who would grow up as he had. But, a year after they started dating, Denice told him that she was pregnant. "I was furious and wanted nothing to do with her. For nine months I said nothing to her, even though she would not leave me alone. She came around my house all the time and made my life miserable!" James complained. His mother and father continually told him that he was treating her wrong and that he needed to help her out, but James was determined that he would not lift a finger to make her life easier. When the baby came, James was 15, and things began to change.

Forced by his parents to see his son, from the first meeting, James knew that he could not abandon him. "He looked just like me, and I got to thinking that I was treating him the same way my dad had treated me. Somehow it just didn't seem fair." In his state he had a legal responsibility to provide whatever money he could to the welfare office, but, coming from a family that was on welfare, he had no job and no extra money. He still had to sign a paper stating that he would provide what he could to support his son. That legal obligation, combined with his mother's insistence that he be responsible, led him to decide that he couldn't just walk away. His mother, brothers, and sisters kept on telling him that this was not the end of the world, offered to help at any time, and encouraged him to keep on trying even when he felt absolutely overwhelmed by all of his responsibilities.

With the assistance of both families, the young couple began to live together, and James, who had been used to looking after his brothers' and sisters' children, assumed the role of father. A gifted athlete and a good student, James was determined to stay in school. His friends gradually quit coming around and frequently he was embarrassed to admit that he had a son. He became well known in his community for his basketball ability and received a full scholarship to a college in another state. Fortunately, the college was located in the town where his girlfriend's parents live, so they had a free place to reside.

"I was determined to succeed for him. I don't blame my parents, but I didn't want him to have the hard life I had. I made myself work to show him that if I could do it, he could too. We were both in school, and he saw me studying and trying to do well in sports. I think some of my motivation rubbed off on him. He's a good student in school and loves sports."

When asked to talk about the most difficult part of this experience, James said that he felt so different from everyone else. Later on, some of his friends found themselves in the same situation. James believes that they quit school so they could go to work and support their children. "They saw how hard I worked to stay in school, and I suppose a few of them tried to do that too. But most of them made a big mistake and dropped out; today they have gotten nowhere and hardly have any contact with their kids. It was hard for me, and sometimes I wanted to hide the fact that I was living with my girl-friend and a father. I got so much attention because of basketball, and I didn't want to tell people. I just kept thinking about my responsibilities to push myself to work harder."

Today, James and Denice are still not married, but they are living together and, now that college is behind them, believe they will marry in the near future. They have not had other children as yet.

Case Discussion

From the factors reviewed, it can be seen that James and Denice had a relationship of some duration, but that it was not initially strong enough to overcome his anger at her for getting pregnant. The relationship was exclusive, they discussed birth control and agreed not to have a baby, but things did not turn out that way. James put the responsibility of contraception squarely on Denice. He used the crisis of his son's birth to push himself to higher levels of success, and also has used his relationship with Denice to build what appears to be a strong family unit. The fact that welfare rules in his state required that he sign a letter of intent to support his child was also a factor in his feeling responsible. Both his family and the state were telling him that he had obligations to his child.

James, like Mike in the case at the beginning of the chapter, was able to use the birth of his son to keep himself focused on success. Being a student, an athlete, and an employee left little time for being a father. But using his extended family as a support base, he made it and today rejoices in his relationship with his son. Other men I interviewed felt the same sense of obligation, but did not have the internal or external resources to maintain their fathering role. James and Mike were fortunate to have a goal that they kept before themselves, and a support network that fostered their efforts to be successful. The following is the case of Thomas, a teenage father who chose a different route.

Thomas: A Forgotten Father

Thomas became a teenage father at 16. His mother had had four children, each with a different father. Men seemed to come and go around his house. He was not really serious about his girlfriend. As a matter of fact, they had not even seen each other for six weeks when she called to tell him she was pregnant. "I'm still not sure that the baby was mine," Thomas said bitterly. He was not ready to commit himself to her because she slept around almost as much as he did. They did not talk about birth control, but sometimes he did use a condom. She did not seem interested in getting more deeply involved with Thomas either since she had a new boyfriend. But Thomas asked her what she wanted him to do, and she said that she hoped he would come when the baby was born. Then he lost contact with her. "She never even called me when he was born, and if I hadn't bumped into them at the mall, I would have never seen my baby. He was real cute, but I didn't want to be involved with her. I asked if I could see him sometimes but she said her boyfriend wouldn't like me hanging around. I just let them go."

Today Thomas is 27 and has been living with a woman for four years. He says they get along, and that he enjoys their daughter who is now 2 years old. "I like being a father to her, and sometimes I wonder what has happened to my son. I play with her and we watch TV together, and I like putting her to bed. She's going to have a better life than I had. We'll probably marry sometime, but I'm not sure when. I don't feel good about leaving my son, but now I've lost him. Maybe one day he will find me and we'll be able to get to know each other."

Case Discussion

Thomas presents a profile of the stereotype of a teenage father who does not get involved with his child. It appears that he does care about his son, but that he sees no future in trying to find him to become a part of his life. He is typical of some of those fathers who are not involved. Others said things like, "He wouldn't want to know me. My life is pretty much of a mess," and "I would not want him to see me now. There's not really anything that I can do well, and I've never had a job for more than a few months. I can hardly look after myself; I don't know what I would do if I had to look after him too." These men simply have so few resources either in terms of self-esteem or finances to take on the responsibility of a child. And they often live in a culture that does not take the father role seriously. Babies seem to belong to their mothers, and fathers just seem to drift away. Our criteria of self-esteem, the nature of the relationship with the woman, the level of commitment, the discussion of possible pregnancy and the use of birth control indicate that Thomas functioned at a low level on each, a predictor that he would not be a highly involved father. Now let's examine one final case before putting Mike, James, and Thomas in perspective.

Richard: Focused on the Future

Richard is 36 years old today and is creating a new relationship with his 17-year-old son, Tony. He and his ex-wife started dating when they were in the eighth grade and never really went out with anyone else. When they became sexually active, she went on birth control pills. Because of negative side effects of the pills, she discontinued them for a short time, and during that time became pregnant. Already engaged, their marriage was not a big surprise to anyone, but as college freshmen, setting up housekeeping did complicate their lives. Richard was able to stay in college, and the birth of his son led their families to become more supportive of their situation. He had little free time but has always been an energetic person, used to a full life. Both of them took great delight in living the suburban dream after he graduated. But he was soon discontent with what he calls "a plastic existence" and decided to go to seminary and give his energy to helping people who live in inner-city disadvantaged neighborhoods. He was accepted into a special program that allowed him to complete the three-year course of study in one year and then accepted a job in a Southern city. During the time he had been in seminary, his wife and son had moved in with her mother and they didn't see much of each other.

According to Richard, "When Tony was born the major thing I needed to make our life work was money. So for the first few years I focused on the provider role, but after a while I got tired of thinking about money so much; my life seemed so empty and I decided to junk everything and start over. Seminary was an intense experience for me, one that did not include time for my family, so they had to go away. During our seven-month separation the cracks that eventually led to our divorce were probably evident. But after I graduated we moved south and became a family again. We separated when Tony was 12 and divorced a couple of years later. Tony chose to live with me, and for a while we got along fine. But he got into drugs and alcohol and refused to go to school so I kicked him out. Now, after a year of being on his own, he has come back home and is ready to get his life in order. When he left I told him to give me the key to the house, but once he began to turn around I gave it back. I'm glad that he's using it now, and I hope that he will get back into school and get a plan set for his life. I'm going to marry again in a few months and will move out of the country. Tony doesn't want to come with us, but he knows that I will help him through school and that he is welcome at any time. In some ways I am a dinosaur, for we got pregnant before abortion was so easy and at a time when single, unmarried parenthood was not socially acceptable. I don't think you will see many young people doing what we did. Today there are just more models other than marriage or abandonment."

Case Discussion

Again, Richard indicates that many of the predictors of father involvement were at work in his situation. He was in an exclusive, committed relationship that had lasted for several years; they did discuss the possibility of pregnancy and decided to use birth control; and they had a social network that supported their marriage. But Richard, like James and Mike, had lots of energy and knew how to focus that energy on achieving his goals. Again we see a young father with clear values, surrounded by a network that encouraged his decision to be an active father, and determined to succeed. The fact that their marriage lasted for almost thirteen years is a source of some pride to Richard, who said, "We almost beat the odds."

Assessment of Teen Fatherhood Experiences on Adult Men's Lives

A common theme that appears in every interview is that these men are very much aware of their children and do not conform to the stereotype of the teenage father who is simply out to have a good time. Even those who do not have contact with their children think about them frequently and do not feel good about having lost them. Marcus said he felt lousy and confused. He said he agonized about leaving. Allan said he felt strange with a baby and embarrassed at times to be married and a father. "I looked awfully young— like a little 14-year-old boy—people thought my little girl was my sister." Of course, it is important to remember that these are just the ten men who came forward and do not represent all adolescent fathers. But what they present is a picture of a man who has strong ties to his child in spite of the difficulties the child presented. In the past, the father's absence has been construed as a sign of uncaring. However, in many of these cases, even though the father was not around, he still felt pain, and the child—and often the mother— remained in his uppermost thoughts.

As a whole, eight of the ten described themselves as only marginally interested in school. Rather than being academically oriented, they were most involved in peer group activities and in relationships with their girlfriends.

Those who finished college or graduate degrees often had to work very hard and did not have much time available to spend with their children. In those instances they believe that their current relationship with their children was enhanced by their extended family's efforts to include the children in family activities rather than simply leaving them to their mother's families.

Among those who married, the marital relationships vary. In most instances, the marriage began to suffer quite early and soon there was little connection between the parents other than the child. One father said, "Once we married and our son was born she just sat around and gained almost a pound a week. I tried to interest her in doing things, but she just wanted to sit there and eat. Pretty soon I asked her to leave." Another father said, "I was planning to marry her anyway. Her being pregnant just gave me an excuse to quit school; I'd never been much of a student anyway. Things went well for the first couple of years, but then we just drifted apart. Pretty soon she was busy with her career and didn't seem interested in me."

Those marriages that have lasted are reported as constantly shaky. Although the couples seem committed to staying together, the men do not report a lot of closeness or much in common. One father who has been married for seventeen years said, "Annie and Mary [his 17-year-old daughter] spend lots of time together, leaving me with our son. I think they would spend every dime I make and still not be satisfied with me. Lots of times I feel like they've ganged up on me, that both of them resent me for her having gotten pregnant." Reasons for staying married included supporting their children and not disappointing their extended families. Their attitude seems to be, "We've made it this far; let's not give up now."

Economically, those with the most education seem to have prospered the most in their adult lives. But this also reflects that they had a support system that encouraged them to stay in school both emotionally and often financially. Their parents were not necessarily wealthy, but they knew the value of education and were determined to see that these young men had the economic benefits of education. It is worth noting that among those men who reported the closest relationship with their children, there were extended families that made constant efforts to include the children in family activities. One father said, "My son lives with his mother in the same town where my parents live. He has a key to their house and goes to all the family events. He is close to his cousins and even has a job in the family business. My mother is the one who has made this happen. He was her first grandchild and has always been special to her." Each father stated that although he did not have much contact with his child's mother, he does not resent her or feel that she stood in the way of his developing a relationship with his child.

The impact of the child on subsequent marriages is evident. Four of the ten men waited several years to marry or remarry and chose wives who are seven to ten years younger than them. Some of them plan on no children and no marriage. Their age difference was reported as a factor that complicated their wives' developing a satisfactory relationship with their husbands' children. Although the wives were not ashamed of their husbands' adolescent parenthood, they were not always eager to become stepmothers and often had a stormy relationship with their husbands' children. This is not unlike the situation faced by the blended families created by more typical means (see, for example, Robinson and Barret 1986).

Looking back at the questions that were raised at the beginning of the chapter, what can one conclude about teenage fathers from these interviews? Most of the men report that the experience of becoming a teenage father was a sobering event. Eight of them continue to be involved with their children and can point to specific ways being a young father changed their lives. The most dramatic is the case of James, who, more than any other father interviewed, used the crisis of his son's birth to inspire himself and others to set and attain goals. Only two of the fathers have lost contact with their children, and in both cases these men had few resources to back them up. Their lives are marked by failure rather than success.

Do fathers maintain contact with their children and ever become custodial parents? In eight of ten cases reviewed, the answer is "yes" to both questions. These men are deeply involved in the father role and have committed themselves to both the delights and the worries of parenthood. Two men talked about their sons as teenagers who have had a difficult time. Besides Richard, one father said that he had also had to kick his son out of the house for drug and alcohol abuse and failure to attend school. One father talked about discussions he had had with his son's high school teachers: "They said he was just like me, never really interested in school, but that he had a good attitude. I wish I had him here with me so maybe I could help him on a daily basis." Comments from other fathers back up their deep concern for their children's welfare. And even those fathers who have had no relationship with their children talk about how their failures would be a disappointment to their sons and daughters.

When it comes to assessing the influence of early fatherhood, the answers are not so clear. Although all of the involved fathers reported strong love for their children, none of them would recommend that teenage fatherhood be an appropriate goal for anyone. Those that turned what could have been a highly negative experience into a success stated that the cost was often high and still a source of bad feelings. Like Mike at the beginning of the chapter, they talk about ways their responsibilities interfered with their being available to their children. One father said, "I knew I was really letting her down by not being around more, and I hated to see her cry when she went back to her mother, but I knew that I had to get back to work if we were ever going to get anywhere." Another said, "It was pitiful to see how he worshipped me. He would follow me around the house refusing to let me out of his sight. But

I was young and just had to get away sometimes. I still worry that I hurt him too much." From talking to these men it is clear that most of them viewed fatherhood as a serious responsibility, one that led them to take life more seriously and one that encouraged them to work harder to succeed.

Although only one of the marriages created by an unplanned teenage pregnancy has endured, seven of the fathers are now married or in relationships that seem headed towards marriage. The father who married at 17 and still lives with that family said, "I'm not sure staying married has been the best thing for any of us. My wife and my daughter often gang up on me and really seem to hate me sometimes. I mostly hang around with my son and work. If it weren't for our families and for the fact that we've been married eighteen years, I would just leave. I don't regret the years I've been married, and often I feel proud that we've managed so well, but I sure do wish I was in a marriage that was happier."

Finally, do the variables that researchers indicate predict father involvement stand up after examining the lives of these fathers? Again, the answer seems to be "yes." Self-esteem, or at least an awareness of one's strengths, seems to enable some young fathers to overcome the hurdles placed before them. The nature of the relationship with the girlfriend is a clear indicator of father involvement. For eight of the ten men interviewed, the pregnancy occurred in a relationship that was long-standing, exclusive, and committed. These couples discussed the possibility of pregnancy and knew how to use birth control. And all of them had social and family support networks that encouraged them to be involved parents. It is significant that when the family network is supportive, the network of friends seems less important. With the practical responsibilities of young parenthood, there is little time or money left for friends, a loss that many of these fathers lamented.

Conclusion

The men whose lives have been encapsulated here have come forward for a variety of reasons. They do not represent all teenage fathers, but they do represent many. The method used to gather data in this chapter is not scientific. Although interesting and in some cases illuminating, these are simply anecdotes drawn from only one part of very complex lives. Still, teenage parenting can have a positive influence on the adult lives of parents. This is not to say that it is appropriate to advocate teenage parenthood, but only that in spite of the many hurdles that must be overcome, some teenage fathers do succeed, both in careers and as parents.

Professionals who work in the area of adolescent pregnancy can do several things to strengthen the involvement of teenage fathers. Making birth control information available to young teenagers is important, but is not sufficient because many pregnancies are a result of contraceptive failure. Schools need to create programs that provide information on intimate relationships and ways to formulate and attain goals. Boys need to have places where they can discuss their relationships with girls and become more aware of the consequences of parenthood at any age. Unfortunately, too many school counselors who could fill this role are burdened with excessive clerical duties that allow them no time for counseling.

Professionals can also routinely include questions about the teenage father when interviewing pregnant adolescents. Simply asking about the boy's involvement and whereabouts is not sufficient. Encouraging the girl to bring the boy in for an interview or arranging activities for expectant teenage fathers during clinic hours will underscore the potential role of the father.

Reaching out to the parents of pregnant teenagers could be one way to activate a network that can be a strong source of support. Training ministers and teachers in ways they can be helpful along with promoting models of father involvement may encourage teen fathers to come forward. Many of them are fatherless themselves and have no idea what it can mean to be a father.

Finally, preaching to teenagers is not going to work. Rather, listening to them talk about what is happening to them while telling them about models is the best approach. Seeking out men as speakers who have succeeded in spite of their young fathering could be a powerful influence on subsequent father behavior. These suggestions will be expounded upon and additional ones discussed in the next chapter.

References

Barret, R.L. & Robinson, B.E. (1982) A descriptive study of teenage expectant fathers. *Family Relations* 31:349–62.

———. (1987) "The role of adolescent fathers in parenting and childrearing." In A.R. Stiffman & R.A. Feldman (eds.), *Advances in adolescent mental health. Vol. IV, Childbearing and childrearing.* Greenwich, Conn.: JAI Press.

Belsky, J. & Miller, B. (1986) "Adolescent fatherhood in the context of the transition to parenthood." In A.B. Elster & M.E. Lamb (eds.), *Adolescent parenthood,* pp. 107–22. Hillsdale, New Jersey: Lawrence Erlbaum.

Herzog, J.M. (1984) "Boys who make babies." In M. Sugar (ed.), *Adolescent parenthood,* pp. 65–74. Jamaica, New York: Spectrum.

Robinson, B.E. & Barret, R.L. (1982) Issues and problems related to the research of teenage fathers: A critical analysis. *Journal of School Health* 52:596–600.

———. (1986) *The developing father.* New York: Guilford Press.

———. (27 May 1987) Myths about adolescent fathers with policy change implications for health care professionals. Paper presented at the Association for the Care of Children's Health 22nd Annual Conference, Halifax, Nova Scotia.

Vinkousis, M.A. (1986) "Young fathers and their children: Some historical and policy perspectives." In A.B. Elster & M.E. Lamb (eds.), *Adolescent parenthood,* pp. 171–92. Hillsdale, New Jersey: Lawrence Erlbaum.

7
Suggestions for Practitioners

> Given the continuing involvement of these [adolescent] fathers with their infants, our exclusion of fathers and our failure to provide educational and social support for paternal roles leave fathers uninformed about infant care, infant competencies, and infant needs.
> —Michael Yogman (1982, p. 268)

Phyllis Mandell (1987), child life coordinator in the pediatric unit of Saint Michael's Medical Center in Newark, New Jersey, listened as 17-year-old Jake told her how hard it was to bring up his daughter. He hadn't expected to be a father—especially the father of a deaf baby girl. He had tried to tell a social worker and a physician but no one would listen to him, so the child went deaf. He explained that at 6 months he noticed she wasn't making any noises, but didn't think anything of it because he didn't know what was "normal." By the time he brought her to the doctor, the damage was irreversible. He was glad to hear about the program, though, and said he wished someone had told him what to expect.

Another incident occurred when Roosevelt, the young father, rushed into the hospital too late to see his dead infant. His child had been critically ill for two weeks but no one had informed him that the baby was sick until after the child had died. The mother had spent nights on end staying with the baby with practically no help at all. Hospital personnel had asked the exhausted mother, "Isn't there anybody else we can call to come help you?"

"No," she replied.

"Are you sure? What about the father?" the practitioner asked.

"Oh, I don't even know where he is. Besides, he doesn't care about us anyway."

When the father got to the hospital, he was very upset that he had not been contacted and that "nobody thought I cared." He was distraught that his baby had died without his being there to grieve the death and to offer his emotional help during his baby's suffering.

Jake and Roosevelt are both victims of a human service system that still doesn't recognize or support teenage fathers. An attentive ear from either the social worker or physician might have saved the infant's hearing as well as given the young father some sense of credibility. An intake system that more assertively involved the teenage father in his offspring's medical services might also have been a comfort for Roosevelt when mourning his baby's death.

Practitioners are always asking what they can do to work better with adolescent parents. My first answer is that, as practitioners, we need to improve our credibility. We need to examine our own sex biases against young fathers and include young fathers in every aspect of service delivery. One social worker from the Children's Home Society in California described an eye-opening experience in this regard:

> I discovered that I was counseling with the expectation that the fathers didn't want to contribute. I wasn't confronted with my own values until I saw some natural fathers who really wanted to get involved, wanted to see their babies and wanted contact with the adopting couples so that they could clarify why they were doing this and prevent distorted information from being passed on. (Connolly 1978, p. 42)

Although casework practices have assumed in the past that teen fathers do not want to be involved in the decision-making process concerning abortion, adoption, or keeping the baby, family scientists have recently found that young expectant fathers, although frightened, want to help make decisions and plans concerning their female partners and their babies (Fry & Trifiletti 1983). This chapter will show how service providers have overlooked needs of teenage fathers and suggest ways in which practitioners who become involved with unwed mothers can extend their services to unwed fathers.

Involving Teenage Fathers

Many teenage fathers do not seek out schoolteachers, the clergy, or social service agencies for help. A study of adolescent fathers in Tulsa, Chicago, and Columbus reported that only two of the ninety-five fathers said they would seek out a social service agency for help, only one young father said he would go to a minister for help, and none said they would go to a schoolteacher for advice or help with their problems (Hendricks, Howard & Caesar 1981).

Hendricks and his associates found that teachers were not used as sources of help because they were not equipped to deal with problems associated with teenage parenthood. Social service agencies and the clergy were not used because proper counseling was not available to the young fathers for making appropriate decisions about such matters as abortion, adoption,

child support, and continuation of schooling. Others who h
issue have suggested that agencies and institutions that serve
needs systematically devalue the male role and exclude male
(Scales 1977). Still others have shown that the helping profess
made an assertive outreach attempt to serve adolescent father
been dubbed "forgotten parents" (Allen-Meares 1984, Barret
1986).

The literature suggests that practitioners who work with unmarried
mothers have not given enough attention to unmarried fathers, except for a
punitive or superficial involvement (Allen-Meares 1984, Robinson & Barret
1986). One study, in fact, concluded that social workers continue to be ambivalent toward including unwed fathers in adoption proceedings and still
view the mother as the main source of nurturance for children (Pierce 1981).

The practitioner's ability to work effectively with teenage fathers is crucial as the numbers of teenage pregnancy cases spiral. Counseling services for
adolescents need to be expanded so that boys who impregnate girls are included in programs of abortion or adoption counseling. The first step is to
carefully monitor any personal prejudices that characterize young fathers as
aloof, unconcerned, and eager to avoid responsibility for involvement in the
pregnancy. Personnel should make sure their agencies involve teenage fathers
in the delivery of services as specified by each state. The attempt to attract
the father is not a simple task. Often these young men are suspicious and may
not come forward unless they are convinced that programs have something to
offer beyond forcing them to assume financial responsibility for their children. Because of their awareness of the negative stereotype associated with
teenage fathers, young men are hesitant to take advantage of programs unless
special efforts are made to reach them.

Suzanne Sgroi (1982) refers to "authoritative intervention" as an effective
means of involving clients in child sexual abuse cases. Although teenage pregnancy is an entirely separate issue with its own set of concerns and problems,
authoritative intervention is frequently necessary when dealing with teenage
fathers. Instead of sitting back, for instance, and waiting for young fathers
to come for help, practitioners must be prepared to go to them.

Vigorous efforts such as sending caseworkers to schools and recreational
facilities where young fathers are likely to "hang out" will spread the word
through informal networks. Contacts in parking lots, pool halls, basketball
courts, barbershops, recreational centers; flyers on windshields at rock con-
certs or midnight movies; and ads on public transportation and displays at
flea markets have been suggested as stronger ways of reaching teenage fathers
and promoting sexual responsibility among adolescent males (Hendricks
1983, McCallister 1979). Public service spots on television or interviews in
newspapers that feature teenage males talking realistically about their experiences as fathers and the help they have received from programs may increase

the likelihood of participation. Such an approach can also create an awareness of the consequences of unprotected intercourse among teenage boys who have not yet become fathers and may encourage them to use birth control to avoid an unwanted pregnancy.

Aggressive outreach for the father also may be necessary during the intake process and in continued work with the mother. Asking teenage mothers to invite the fathers of their babies is sometimes the first step. Once young fathers become involved, they must be encouraged to share their needs and participate in decision-making. Simply by understanding that adolescent fathers are as needy as young mothers, workers can provide more equitable services to teen parents as a whole and even more importantly to the children. Efforts to include fathers in services to mothers are more likely to ensure the father's long-term active and responsible participation in the care of his offspring (Parke, Power & Fisher 1980). Involvement of the prospective father in the pregnancy may not only be supportive to the mother, but may have potential benefits to the child (Vaz, Smolen & Miller 1983). On the other hand, the failure of medical and social services to actively involve the adolescent father may result in a decrease in regular contact between him and the mother after the second postnatal year (Barret & Robinson 1985).

Theoretical Guides

In choosing theoretical guides for helping teenage fathers, family counselors, social workers, and other therapists must continue to explore alternatives to Freudian theory, which emphasizes pathological behavior. Clearly, antiquated Freudian themes continue to dominate the thinking of many practitioners as reflected through their professional literature. Note, for example, this recent comment from the Group for the Advancement of Psychiatry (1986):

> Teenage boys are not immune from analogous fantasies about pregnancy, childbirth, and infants. They, too, identify with infants in positive or envious and rivalrous ways. They may equate impregnating a girl with winning out over other males, though rivalry often involves only the ability to have sexual intercourse and to satisfy a woman. Many boys equate manhood with fathering a child; this leads to using girls for self-affirming purposes. (p. 12)

Reading this psychoanalytic interpretation causes one to wonder if practitioners have really advanced in their thinking of adolescent pregnancy over the past forty years. Such armchair interpretations are unproductive in coming to grips with the adolescent pregnancy issues of the 1980s. These ivory-tower imaginings can only restrain us from advancing in solving today's real-life problems of adolescent pregnancy. The profession must rid itself of such stereotypical interpretations of teenage fathers for which there is not one shred of scientific evidence.

Simplistic Freudian explanations of the 1940s will not work in our complex society of the 1980s. More likely there are multiple reasons for teenage pregnancy that can only be understood and addressed through an ecological approach. Helping professionals must consider the many factors that impact on young boys that lead to premature pregnancy by taking a comprehensive view of the whole person interacting with, not just responding to, the surrounding environment. This is possible through a systems framework, as suggested by Urie Bronfenbrenner (1979).

The young father has his own developmental level that must be considered as it interrelates with the environmental forces that influence this development. Adolescent males, for example, tend to be idealistic in their thinking and often believe what happens to other adolescents can never happen to them. They are also struggling with forming their own identities and figuring out the course of their adult lives.

Adolescent males who live in poverty, who are performing poorly in school, and who have role models of early pregnancies may view early fatherhood as a normative cultural experience that gives them some means of identity and role clarification (Rivara, Sweeney & Henderson 1985). By examining the developmental role conflict that teenage males face when fatherhood is imminent, service providers can help them manage the simultaneous crises of adolescence, pregnancy, prospective parenthood, and sometimes marriage.

By intervening at the family, school, and governmental levels, practitioners will be able to have a greater impact on these young men. Conceptualizing the prospective young father as a system influenced by many personal, human, and environmental factors, workers can bring more appropriate solutions to bear on the problem. Both sets of grandparents, the young father and mother, and peers are all resources that can be utilized in the prevention and intervention processes.

Sex Education and Family Life Planning

Sex education and family life planning are two preventive approaches that practitioners can take to teenage pregnancy. Counselors and teachers in public schools can work together to develop programs for males and females in family life education, sociology, psychology, and home economics that provide information on human reproduction, contraception, parenting, and family planning. Caseworkers can collaborate with school counselors to create imaginative programs that serve all school-age youth.

Sex Education

Research indicates that 95 percent of the adolescent fathers would be interested in receiving services from a teenage parenting agency. Sex education was at the top of their list of needs along with job training, job placement, and parenting information (Hendricks 1980). Primary prevention of teenage fatherhood, however, requires interrupting the sequence of steps leading to parenthood before it occurs. The best option is to advocate for sex education in the early grades before children become sexually active, so they can make more responsible decisions regarding their sexual behavior. Breaking the cycle of adolescent pregnancy begins in early childhood, when sex education should be an integral part of the curriculum. It should be integrated in a developmentally appropriate way from kindergarten through high school. C. Everett Koop (1987), the U.S. Surgeon General, agrees with early instruction:

> Before AIDS education begins, a child should be given information relative to his or her own sexuality. And instead of calling it "sex education," I'd like it called something like studies of human development. I think children should be learning all about themselves, their unbelievable complexity, and especially of their own great value. If they are properly taught their own worth, we can expect them to treat themselves and others with great respect. Human development instruction should keep pace with—and not anticipate—their individual development and curiosity.

Parents of kindergarteners must be simultaneously helped to know how understanding sex and sexuality is a developmental task, just as understanding math or the English language is. Foundations must be built in the early years rather than suddenly thrust upon adolescents in an awkward and uncomfortable way.

Of course, sex education becomes most crucial during adolescence, when teenagers become sexual beings both biologically and socially. As I discussed earlier, large numbers of teenage males are sexually active without benefit of contraception and contraceptive services. Some of these males may need more information about effective contraception and how contraception can be obtained. Others may need more convincing about the necessity of contraceptive responsibility (Sonenstein 1986).

Health care practitioners who work with adolescents must be adequately trained to counsel them on sexual matters and specific contraceptive methods for those who request it. Because no one method is best for all, it has been suggested that practitioners take a "cafeteria" or "supermarket" style approach in presenting a variety of birth control options (Greydanus 1982).

To achieve successful sex education programs, practitioners must help teenage males and females to assume responsibility for contraceptive decisions. With an awareness of the accessibility and effectiveness of various birth control methods, adolescents have a greater chance of avoiding unwanted and unplanned pregnancies (Hewson 1986). The majority of teen pregnancy programs, however, focus on female adolescents with the implicit assumption that females are more responsible for contraception than males (Sheehan, Ostwald & Rothenberger 1986), despite evidence that adolescents perceive birth control to be a shared responsibility. It is essential that practitioners reconsider sex education curriculum for adolescents and present a more balanced, egalitarian view in which responsibility can be jointly shared and concerns of both sexes can be addressed (Sheehan, Ostwald & Rothenberger 1986). For those interested in establishing a sex education course, a format and directions for instructors are presented in box 7–1.

Family Life Education

Programs in human sexuality should, of course, deal with more than reproductive physiology and aspects of contraception. They can deal with the emotional response of both males and females to pregnancy and emphasize the young father's often intense involvement in the pregnancy. They also can focus more generally on the whole person, family life, and human communication and feelings.

These programs should be comprehensive enough to help young children and teenagers build positive self-concepts and feelings of self-worth and an understanding of the consequences of teenage parenthood. Programs at the junior and senior high school levels teach youth about how the family functions as a system and how each member influences and is influenced by the system. The role of interpersonal communication is underscored as students actively participate in simulations of marriage, childbirth, separation, divorce, and many of the issues that couples face in today's world (Black & DeBlassie 1985).

Schools and churches are a natural place for parent education programs for parents of all ages as well as for youth who one day will be parents. Professionals can capitalize on the parents' continued influence on their adolescents (Flick 1986). Special parent programs or groups composed of parents and their teenagers could be established where honest, straightforward communication would be assured. Parents and their teenagers can become better informed and comfortable with talking about sexuality and contraception.

Box 7–1
Format for Sex Education Course and Directions for Instructors*

Week 1: *Introduction*. Inform students about the course's contents, requirements, and goals, and answer questions. Administer the pretest. Collect note cards with questions about topics of major concern to the students.

Week 2: *Group Discussion:* Discuss the questions submitted by the students.

Week 3–5: *Anatomy and Physiology*. Have clinic personnel and experts teach this part. Use visual aids.

Week 6: *Contraceptives*. Begin with a discussion of examples of contraceptives. Arrange for clinic personnel to discuss access to contraceptives.

Week 7: *Egg-carrying project*. Give one raw egg to each student. Instruct the students to bring the egg each week for the next 4 weeks and to keep a diary of their feelings about carrying the egg. (This exercise is designed to impress upon adolescents the fragility of the egg and about the care and time involved in carrying it.)

Week 8: *Sexually transmitted diseases*. Discuss the kinds, modes of transmission, symptoms, and treatment of sexually transmitted diseases, including AIDS.

Week 9: *Services available in the community and adolescent clinic*. Inform the students about the kinds, functions, and coordination of available services. Invite a clinic staff person to discuss the clinic's services. Administer a test (optional) based on the material covered during weeks 3–9.

Week 10: *Group Discussion*. Collect the students' diaries on the egg-carrying project. Discuss the similarities between the egg and caring for an infant, the realities of caring for a child and its effect on an adolescent's life. Discuss the responsibility for another's life—and how little an adolescent will be able to provide for an infant.

Week 11: *Group Discussion*. In a round-table setting, moderate a discussion of what factors will help to provide and detract from each of the course's goals.

Week 12: *Conclusion*. Discuss the results of the pretest and posttest. Address topics that were incorrectly answered on the posttest. Summarize the course, emphasizing the salient points. Discuss extracurricular projects that students will do for 4 weeks.

Weeks 13–17: *Extracurricular projects*. The students are to participate in activities such as those mentioned earlier (helping mothers to care for infants and so forth).

Week 18: *Final group discussion*. Informally discuss the outcomes of the projects. (The purpose of this session is to maintain contact with the students.)

---

*Reprinted from Dipali Apte (1987, January–February) A plan to prevent adolescent pregnancy and reduce infant mortality. *Public Health Reports* 102:84. Used with permission.

Social Support Networks

One of the biggest obstacles young fathers face is a lack of support (real or imagined) from those around them. Practitioners can alleviate feelings of isolation and depression by establishing social networks for teenage fathers or taking advantage of those already in place. Paternal grandparents, peers, and the media are three major support systems that can be utilized.

Paternal Grandparents

The state of Wisconsin recently passed legislation making grandparents financially responsible for the offspring of their teenage children. Despite this punitive approach to the utilization of grandparents, research suggests that grandparents of the baby—especially the father's parents—are untapped and useful sources of social support for these young men (Allen-Meares 1984). Asked, "Who would you go to first with a problem?" 70 percent of one group of teenage fathers said their mothers above anyone else (Hendricks 1980). They also reported being closer to their mothers when they were growing up. Unfortunately, the involvement of the paternal grandmother and grandfather in adolescent pregnancies is more the exception than the norm. Allen-Meares (1984) suggests that by ignoring the adolescent father and his parents, service providers could be ignoring the emotional needs of fathers and undermining a potential support system for the adolescent mother and baby. On the other hand, involvement of paternal grandparents allows them to become part of a natural support system that can eliminate some of the negative consequences of teenage parenting.

Maternal grandmothers are also valuable sources of support. In many cases they become the infant's primary caregiver while the mother works or returns to school. In fact, Furstenburg (1976) reported that only 5 percent of his group of mothers were primary caretakers of their babies.

Family groups composed of both sets of grandparents and the adolescent parents can be useful in conflict resolution. Maternal grandparents can vent the often-expressed feelings that the boy has violated their daughter and ruined her life. Paternal grandparents can reveal any hidden resentments toward the adolescent mother. Resentments from grandparents can prolong the adolescent pregnancy crisis, delay the necessary decision making, and ultimately harm the baby as well (Allen-Meares 1984).

Peer Support

Surprisingly, the literature suggests that adolescent fathers do not perceive their peers as sources of social support. Interview data indicate that the average teenage father gets no support from his peers when faced with an unplanned and unwanted pregnancy (Fry & Trifiletti 1983): "He is told to keep cool by his friends if he is anxious to talk with them about his fears. Also, these fathers perceive anyone wanting to contact them as 'being after them'" (p. 226).

Hendricks (1980) found that, although peers were rejected as possible sources of social support, most teen fathers did not feel rejected by their peers. Instead, he concluded that friends could be instrumental in providing proper social support, especially within a well-planned framework in a professional setting.

Practitioners can capitalize on the peer support system that is so important during adolescence. Sometimes, in fact, adolescents will listen to their peers before they will other adults. This can take the form of arranging informal meetings between two fathers or setting up ongoing support groups composed of several fathers. Peer support groups can be structured where teenagers have a platform for speaking openly and frankly about sexual matters. Experienced teen fathers who have suffered the emotional, educational, and financial aftereffects of early parenthood can be resources for classrooms or for groups of young adolescents before a pregnancy occurs. One adolescent father told me:

> If I had it to do all over again, I'd use two rubbers instead of one. The thing that is hard is having to go to work and when you want to come home and relax a little bit you got babies crawling all over you and crying. You just don't get enough time to yourself. That's about my only complaint. It's just not having enough time to do the things I want to do like play golf, basketball, and extracurricular activities. I just don't have time to do them anymore. Be prepared for a lot of long nights. It's not easy. People just don't realize how it changes your life. Just one little girl changes your life 100 percent. Nothing's the same anymore. It's just not the same as it used to be. The baby is always there and you can't run from that.

Sometimes seeing and hearing firsthand from his peers has the effect of lessening the personal fable and laying a potential problem at each adolescent's doorstep. These support groups could also help adolescents identify and examine peer pressure and learn ways of resisting pressure to engage in early sexual activity.

Special groups can be formed for small numbers of teenage males who have already fathered children. These groups allow the young men to share their pain, failures, joys, and successes and can be helpful, especially during times of isolation and rejection by friends, families, and social agencies. Such groups also send messages to teenage males that "you are not alone." Herzog (1984) described the nature of a support group of six sexually active junior and senior high boys—some of whom were fathers—over a four-year period.

The mood of the group ranged from anger, to lighthearted jokes about shotgun weddings, to tears and sadness. Frivolous and cavalier attitudes on the surface often masked inner pain and fears for the benefit of the peer group. Most importantly, teenage fathers provided a system of support and helped one another understand and cope with situational stresses by expressing their emotions in direct ways and in a safe and supportive setting.

A 19-year-old father named Dennis said he wished there were more support groups for married adolescent couples:

> I believe there ought to be some type of counseling to help young couples learn to cope with the new baby because there's a lot of new changes that you're not aware of because they hit you right in the face. That causes a lot of problems sometimes. Another thing would be to have some kind of group meetings of all teen parents because there's not that many young parents around these days. Most of my friends are still running around to the bars and we don't have anything much in common with the people around us that have children. And that would give us a chance to meet some people our same age with the same interests.

While simultaneously taking advantage of the peer support system, practitioners must also remember that sometimes young men need protection from it. Because peers have such an impact on thoughts and behaviors in adolescence—especially in the arena of sexual activity—practitioners should help teenage males identify and examine peer pressure and explore ways to make individual, deliberate decisions (Flick 1986).

Media

Information disseminated to teenage fathers can be a consolation. Newsletters and other periodicals published by national or local organizations and books on adolescent pregnancy written especially for teens can also be a source of support for young fathers and may prevent feelings of isolation. A small library with appropriate reading material available to teens can be arranged in any waiting room, office, lounge, or classroom. Easily read materials often include topics of sex, reproduction, contraception, and the responsibilities of parenthood. Other media such as filmed vignettes or videotapes can be useful tools for helping fathers express and deal with situations that often emerge during the pregnancy experience. Vignettes can be effective because they trigger reactions to experiences of fathers that are similar to those in the films and promote discussion. Films for adolescents can also be shown to grandparents to help them understand their children's experiences. The resources provided in chapter 9 include names of films, organizations and their publications, and other literature written for adults as well as teenagers.

Counseling Needs

The counseling needs of adolescent fathers are multiple and varied. Needs are also closely aligned with the specific point in time of pregnancy and childbirth and the father's age. Programs that are carefully designed with the needs of teenage fathers in mind will also serve as "attractors" for these males (Barret & Robinson 1987). By addressing the young father's emotional needs, professionals can prepare him and his parents for meaningful roles during pregnancy and after the baby is born.

Prenatal Phase

Generally, young expectant fathers need attention immediately upon receiving news of the pregnancy. Practitioners who routinely work with teenage males should be sensitive to signs that might indicate a young male is struggling with news of a pregnancy. Extreme changes in behavior such as sudden withdrawal or acting out, depending upon the general nature of his personality, are a major cue of stress. A sudden drop in school grades or pronounced signs of depression also are indicators to look for. Young fathers may need help with their feelings of shock, fear, and confusion regarding impending fatherhood and in coping with reactions from family and friends. Vaz, Smolen, and Miller (1983) found that the teenage fathers at greatest risk for depression were those who seemed uncertain of which choice to make regarding the pregnancy (to keep the baby, abort, or put the baby up for adoption). Depressed fathers were less likely to be maintaining an ongoing relationship with the prospective mother and were more likely to have known her for less than a year, be in school, and feel that their girlfriend's family's attitude toward them had deteriorated since the pregnancy.

Service providers must be prepared to help young fathers deal with such depression, isolation, and alienation resulting from out-of-wedlock births, decisions to abort, or putting the child up for adoption. Involvement of teenage fathers, however, should not be confused with marriage. Services to prospective fathers should not be contingent upon his willingness to marry, although some programs have advocated male involvement only in instances where the mother plans to marry the teenage father (Lorenzi, Klerman & Jekel 1977). Marriage is not a long-term solution to unwed adolescent pregnancy. As discussed in chapter 3, statistics show that teen marriages fail at alarming rates and young parents find themselves in the wake of educational and financial hardships and often on welfare.

A major role of the practitioner in the prenatal phase is to help the couple and their families decide on a mutually-agreeable course of action. Promoting dialogue between teen parents is essential for planning the father's role in pregnancy, childbirth, and postpartum arrangements; his participation in decisions about the baby; and clarifying mutual expectations about the couple's relationship and child care arrangements (Panzarine & Elster 1982). Equally important is the role of fostering decision making while acting as an advocate for *both* young parents and the unborn child (Allen-Meares 1984). Some medical professionals refer to "supportive care" in which workers express interest and concern to both members of the couple rather than discrimination between young mothers and fathers and encourage the verbalization of questions and fears (Panzarine & Elster 1982). They also recommend the use of "anticipatory guidance" for teenage fathers in this phase of treatment to assuage anxiety and feelings of helplessness. Such guidance involves dissemination of pertinent information regarding pregnancy, labor, delivery, and the father's role during and after childbirth. Experiential involvement such as listening to the baby's heartbeat, feeling fetal movement, or learning fetal parts of the body raise interest and awareness. Physical and emotional changes on the part of both parents alerts them on what to expect from each other.

Practitioners can dispense information on prenatal care, nutrition, and childrearing to teenage parents or refer them to appropriate channels. Health problems or deaths of infants can be decreased when adolescent mothers and fathers receive adequate prenatal care and nutrition. In short, fathers should be given the opportunity to participate in all aspects of the pregnancy experience from prenatal education classes, labor and delivery, to childrearing after the baby is born.

Postnatal Phase

In situations where the decision is to keep the baby and teenage fathers are involved in the daily care of the child, professionals can provide information on child development and care. In those rare circumstances where teenage fathers gain sole custody, parent education is essential to reduce the risk to children. A number of studies indicate that parenting classes and child development information should be targeted at teen fathers as well as teen mothers because of their poor understanding of the nature of children, childrearing, and parenthood (de Lissovoy 1973; Hendricks, Howard & Caesar 1981; Rivara, Sweeney & Henderson 1986). Information about normal infant development will help them have more realistic expectations about their children and themselves as parents, creating situations where the likelihood of child abuse may be lessened. Emphasis can be placed on developing disciplinary styles appropriate to the ages of their children. Teaching communication can also help young fathers be more successful as they interact with their children, girlfriends, and extended families.

Service providers should also encourage adolescent parents to participate in home-based infant stimulation programs designed to educate teens about parenthood, decrease isolation, and encourage the infant's development. Research indicates dramatic positive benefits for babies enrolled in these programs (Field et al. 1980). There are indications that these programs can be beneficial to both mothers and fathers. In one study social workers paid weekly visits to the homes of adolescent mothers and instructed and guided them in infant care techniques for two years (Scarr-Salapatek & Williams 1973). Mothers were interested in the social worker's help and sought their advice on personal problems, feelings of depression, and infant care.

Teenage fathers need encouragement to remain in school and information about places to acquire the skills that will enable them to avoid unfulfilling, monotonous, dead-end jobs. Vocational counseling can assist them in making informed educational and vocational choices about jobs so that they can realize their desire to provide for their children. Where marriages occur, teen parents need continued support for the stresses they encounter. The personal, social, and economic frustrations of married teenage couples contribute to disenchantment in their marriages and negatively influence their interactions with their children (de Lissovoy 1973). Personal counseling through community social services or through adult education classes could help married couples cope with these frustrations in a constructive way.

Regardless of marital status, second-time pregnancies are common among adolescent couples. Even after fathering children, some teenage males hold myths about the possibilities of conception and contraception. Teen fathers need information on contraception and family planning to prevent future unwanted pregnancies.

Age of Father

I have indicated throughout this book that teenagers are not a homogeneous group for whom we can make sweeping recommendations. Aside from cultural and socioeconomic differences, research has shown that age is an important distinguishing factor within this population. A 14-year-old male, for example, is cognitively and emotionally different from a 19-year-old. The older adolescents are at first intercourse, the more likely they are to use contraception (Sonenstein 1986). Younger teenagers are less likely than older ones to become involved or to continue in contraceptive programs or to be effective users of birth control (Philliber, Namerow, & Jones 1985). Consequently, service providers should always keep in mind the diversity of their adolescent clients and make special provisions for those under age 15 who may need more individual attention and one-to-one counseling (Black & De-Blassie 1985; Philliber, Namerow & Jones 1985).

A second consideration is reaching older adult fathers who are partners of adolescent females when considering measures to prevent teenage pregnancy. Research indicates that half of the babies born to teenage mothers are fathered by men over 20 years old (Sonenstein 1986). Although most practitioners aim their energies at high school-age males, they must not overlook those older males who also need services (Nakashima & Camp 1984).

Conclusion

Practitioners play a big role in involving teenage fathers in the lives of their infants and in helping adolescent males cope with the difficult situations in which they find themselves. Outreach programs to young fathers have demonstrated that, once involved, many males are eager to become more competent and caring parents.

Service providers who routinely encounter teenage pregnancy will find their work enhanced once efforts to reach adolescent fathers begin to succeed. Given the opportunity, young men often choose to participate in childbirth and seek information about prenatal and postnatal development and parenting. Personal counseling will help them deal with the stresses accompanying both prenatal and postnatal periods and can help them integrate their adult responsibilities with their normal adolescent needs. Reaching out to teenage fathers has advantages for the total family system. Most of all the babies benefit directly and indirectly. Young men will come forward once they trust the sincerity of the practitioner.

References

Allen-Meares, P. (1984) Adolescent pregnancy and parenting: The forgotten adolescent father and his parents. *Journal of Social Work and Human Sexuality* 3:27–38.

Apte, D.V. (1987) A plan to prevent adolescent pregnancy and reduce infant mortality. *Public Health Reports* 102:80–86.

Barret, R.L., & Robinson, B.E. (1985) "The adolescent father." In S. Hansen & F. Bozett (eds.), *Dimensions of fatherhood*. Beverly Hills, Ca.: Sage.

———. (1986) Adolescent fathers: Often forgotten parents. *Pediatric Nursing* 12: 273–77.

———. (1987) "The role of adolescent fathers in parenting and childrearing." In A.R. Stiffman & R.A. Feldman (eds.), *Advances in adolescent mental health. Vol. IV, Childbearing and childrearing*. Greenwich, Conn.: JAI Press.

Black, C., & DeBlassie, R.R. (1985) Adolescent pregnancy: Contributing factors, consequences, treatment, and plausible solutions. *Adolescence* 20:281–90.

Bronfenbrenner, U. (1979) *The ecology of human development*. Cambridge: Harvard University Press.

Connolly, L. (1978) Boy fathers. *Human Behavior*:40–43.

de Lissovoy, V. (1973) Child care by adolescent parents. *Children Today* 2:22–25.

Field, T., Widmayer, S.M., Stringer, S., & Ignatoff, E. (1980) Teenage, lower-class black mothers and their preterm infants: An intervention and developmental follow-up. *Child Development* 51:426–36.

Flick, L.H. (1986) Paths to adolescent parenthood: Implications for prevention. *Public Health Reports* 101:132–47.

Fry, P.S., & Trifiletti, R.J. (1983) Teenage fathers: An exploration of their developmental needs and anxieties and the implications for clinical-social intervention services. *Journal of Psychiatric Treatment and Evaluation* 5:219–27.

Furstenburg, F.F. (1976) *Unplanned parenthood: The social consequences of teenage childbearing*. New York: The Free Press.

Greydanus, D.E. (1982) "Alternatives to adolescent pregnancy: Review of contraceptive literature." In E.R. McAnarney (ed.), *Premature adolescent pregnancy and parenthood*. New York: Grune & Stratton.

Group for the Advancement of Psychiatry. (1986) *Teenage pregnancy: Impact on adolescent development*. New York: Brunner/Mazel.

Hendricks, L.E. (1980) Unwed adolescent fathers: Problems they face and their sources of social support. *Adolescence* 15:861–69.

———. (1983) Suggestions for reaching unmarried black adolescent fathers. *Child Welfare* 62:141–46.

Hendricks, L.E., Howard, C.S., & Caesar, P.P. (1981) Help-seeking behavior among select populations of black unmarried adolescent fathers: Implications for human service agencies. *American Journal of Public Health* 71:733–35.

Herzog, J.M. (1984) "Boys who make babies." In M. Sugar (ed.), *Adolescent parenthood*. New York: Spectrum Publications.

Hewson, P.M. (1986) Current research on adolescent male attitudes about contraceptives. *Pediatric Nursing* 12:33–37.

Koop, C.E. (1987, April). A surgeon general's prescription for AIDS. Speech presented at the National School Boards Association.

Lorenzi, M.E., Klerman, L.V., & Jekel, J.F. (1977). School-age parents: How permanent a relationship? *Adolescence* 12:13–22.

Mandell, P. (27 May 1987) When parents and patients are one and the same: An approach to teenage parents. Paper presented at the Annual Conference of the Association for the Care of Children's Health, Halifax, Nova Scotia.

McCallister, S. (1979, October). Promoting adolescent male sexual responsibility. Paper presented at the Snow/WACSAP Conference, Washington, D.C.

Nakashima, I.I., & Camp, B.W. (1984) Fathers of infants born to adolescent mothers. *American Journal of Diseases of Children,* 138:452–54.

Panzarine, S., & Elster, A.B. (1982) Prospective adolescent fathers: Stresses during pregnancy and implications for nursing interventions. *Journal of Psychosocial Nursing and Mental Health Services* 20:21–24.

Parke, R.D., Power, T.G., & Fisher, T. (1980) The adolescent father's impact on the mother and child. *Journal of Social Issues,* 36:88–106.

Philliber, S.G., Namerow, P.B., Jones, J.E. (1985) Age variation in use of a contraceptive service by adolescents. *Public Health Reports* 100:34–40.

Pierce, A.D. (1981) Adoption policy and the "unwed father": An exploratory study of social worker response to changing conceptions of fatherhood. *Dissertation Abstracts International* 42:387A.

Rivara, F.P., Sweeney, P.J., & Henderson, B.F. (1985) A study of low socioeconomic status black teenage fathers and their nonfather peers. *Pediatrics* 75:648–56.

———. (1986) Black teenage fathers: What happens when the child is born? *Pediatrics* 78:151–58.

Robinson, B.E., & Barret, R.L. (1986) *The developing father: Emerging roles in contemporary society.* New York: Guilford Press.

Scales, P. (1977) Males and morals: Teenage contraceptive behavior amid the double standard. *The Family Coordinator* 26:211–22.

Scarr-Salapatek, S., & Williams, M.L. (1973) The effects of early stimulation on low-birth weight infants. *Child Development* 44:94–101.

Sgroi, S. (1982) *Handbook of clinical intervention in child sexual abuse.* Lexington, Mass.: Lexington Books.

Sheehan, M.K., Ostwald, S.K., & Rothenberger, J. (1986) Perceptions of sexual responsibility: Do young men and women agree? *Pediatric Nursing* 12:17–21.

Sonenstein, F.L. (1986) "Risking paternity: Sex and contraception among adolescent males." In A.B. Elster & M. Lamb (eds.), *Adolescent fatherhood,* pp. 31–54. Hillsdale, New Jersey: Lawrence Erlbaum.

Vaz, R., Smolen, P., & Miller, C. (1983) Adolescent pregnancy: Involvement of the male partner. *Journal of Adolescent Health Care* 4:246–50.

8
Program Development for Teenage Fathers

Program providers, planners and policy makers must acknowledge, support, and create approaches that bring him [the teen father] and, when appropriate, his parents into the service plan.
—Paula Allen-Meares (1984, p. 32).

In an issue of the Male Involvement Bulletin, *the Center for Population Options describes an innovative health facility. According to the Center:*

The Young Men's Clinic at New York's Columbia Presbyterian Hospital, located in the predominantly Hispanic Washington Heights area, includes an important community education and outreach component in its services. The clinic works closely with other community agencies, from the neighborhood high school and various youth groups, to the basketball courts and the street corners popular among breakdancers. Police officers from the nearby 34th Precinct drop by the clinic and talk with boys about careers in the police force. The clinic cosponsors a summer basketball tournament, supplying tee-shirts to the participants. Staff take a video camera to community agencies that train adolescents in employment skills and tape boys practicing interview skills, at the same time promoting the clinic and sexual responsibility.

Clinic staff also use the video equipment as an innovative technique to bring boys into the Monday night clinic sessions. Staff take the camera out onto the streets and basketball courts and tape boys breakdancing and playing basketball. They talk to the boys about health and sexuality and tell them to come to the clinic on Monday night to see the videotapes and talk more. At the clinic, the boys watch the tapes, talk to counselors, often get physical exams, and learn more about health and sexuality. The subtheme to these techniques, however, is to tap creatively all the resources a neighborhood has to offer to make the clinic and its messages visible in the community (Casey 1986, p.3).

The Young Men's Clinic at Columbia Presbyterian Hospital is a diamond in the rough. It is one of the few new programs designed exclusively for teenage fathers or adolescent males at high risk for fathering in their teens. Such creative and individualized approaches that are tailored to the needs of males, rather than mechanical duplications of programs for teen mothers, are needed if this country is to lower its teenage pregnancy rate.

Historically, programs for school-age parents have been directed toward adolescent mothers and have involved remedial rather than preventive efforts. Most of these programs have emphasized counseling, special education, instruction on prenatal and postnatal nutrition, and special health classes for pregnant female adolescents, whereas contraception and sex education have been given low priority nationwide (Goldstein & Wallace 1978). Program development for teen fathers has followed this trend, stressing intervention after the fact rather than prevention before unwanted pregnancies occur. It is obvious from earlier chapters that the adolescent father is equally at risk for teenage pregnancy as the mother and that both intervention and prevention strategies are needed where he is concerned. Yet he and his family have been grossly overlooked in service delivery practices.

The frequency of contact between mother and father and the important role fathers play in child development have strong implications for program design that can capitalize on existing networks of affiliation (Washington & Rosser 1981). Inclusion of fathers in programs for teenage mothers involves changes in professional wisdom and legislative, social, and welfare policies that, largely, discourage the fathers' participation and accord them no role in child development.

The Missing Link

Some of the maternal pregnancy programs have opened their doors to fathers, albeit halfheartedly, although others continue to focus only on the mother. A recent description of a program for adolescent mothers, for example, purports to discuss elements of successful school-age parenting programs and speculates on the future of families created by teenage parents (Knowles & Tripple 1986). In fact the program never mentions the teen father at all, except in closing remarks that recommend helping "teenage males achieve a more mature approach toward sexuality and parenthood." (Knowles & Tripple 1986, p. 28).

Other programs have been more enthusiastic in their inclusion of adolescent fathers. The Char-Em. Alternative Program in Ann Arbor, Michigan extended its services in 1979 to reach teenage fathers through parental child preparation classes and instruction on child care techniques. A special day for fathers was established and follow-up telephone calls provided many males the encouragement they needed to become involved. The Michigan Concerned with School-Aged Parents (MACSAP) program in Lansing also includes teenage fathers in its services to expectant mothers. The program provides personal counseling, classes in birth techniques, and advice on family planning. In Cleveland, Ohio, the Teen Father Program at Hough-Norwood Youth Services helps teenage fathers stay more involved with their children and become more supportive of the children's mother.

Still, research indicates that adolescent maternity programs featuring services for the father of the baby are exceptions rather than the rule. A national survey queried health officials and school administrators in 125 cities to determine the prevalence of service programs for pregnant teens. Although special programs were offered in 107 cities, less than half (only 49 out of 107 cities) included service programs for the father of the baby (Goldstein & Wallace 1978). Ernie Peacock, coordinator of Project MARCH in Philadelphia, says that in our society men are supposed to have all the answers and that this myth carries down to teenage males as well. "Unfortunately they don't. Yet we continue to expect them to assume responsibility for their sexual behavior, when in fact, they are inadequately prepared to do so."

Increasingly, advocates for teen fathers have cited gender bias as a roadblock that strangles program development and service delivery systems—even when fathers acknowledge paternity, express a desire to participate in the parenting process, and maintain contact with the mother (Allen-Meares 1984, Brown 1983). Many practitioners, including social workers, remain ambivalent toward including unwed fathers in adoption proceedings and continue to view the mother as the main nurturer of children (Pierce 1981). Bolton (1980) calls the exclusion of fathers from program services "thoughtless at best and potentially destructive at worst" (p. 218). Until services include the male partner, prevention efforts will only be minimally successful. Programs that fail to reach out to young fathers not only ignore their emotional needs, but also eliminate a significant support system for the mother and baby. The failure of medical and social services to actively involve the adolescent father may result in a decrease in regular contact between him and the mother after the second postnatal year (Earls & Siegel 1980). In contrast, research suggests that when fathers are integrated into service delivery, they become more involved and provide an integral support system—emotionally and financially—for mother and baby (Furstenburg 1976; Furstenburg, Brooks-Gunn & Morgan 1987). Young fathers also become the recipients of emotional support for their feelings and therefore risks of repeated teen pregnancies are more likely to be reduced (Elster & Panzarine 1979).

Model Intervention Programs

Intervention programs are those aimed at teenage males who have already become or will soon become fathers. These programs generally include efforts to help young men cope as competently as possible in this difficult role.

Goals usually include vocational and educational assistance, child care and parenting information, and even emphasis of the teen father's parental and legal rights. This section is exemplary rather than comprehensive. It presents examples of model programs without attempting to include every such program in existence. Programs are numerous and varied, as they should be, since no single solution to the adolescent pregnancy problem exists.

Teen Father Collaboration Project

In the most widespread initiative of its kind, the Teen Parent Collaboration Project, administered by the Bank Street College of Education in New York City, coordinates services to teenage couples in eight cities across the United States: San Francisco; Philadelphia; Minneapolis; Portland, Oregon; Bridgeport, Connecticut; St. Paul; Poughkeepsie, New York; and Louisville, Kentucky (Klinman 1984). As part of this collaboration, San Francisco's Teenage Pregnancy and Parenting Project teaches adolescent fathers how to change, feed, and hold their babies. At the same time the young men train in a trade and finish school, increasing the likelihood that they will find a job and decreasing the possibility that they will become involved in repeat pregnancies. Peer counselors are on hand to lead discussion groups of young fathers who convene periodically.

Coed classes in natural childbirth and bottle-feeding are held in Philadelphia at the Medical College of Pennsylvania Hospital as part of the Teen Father Program there. Sometimes teen dads participate in childbirth and after delivery they receive instruction in infant care, child development, and family planning.

The Teen Indian Parents Program in Minneapolis provides teenage fathers with instruction on how to play with their infants as well as information on nutrition, parenting, and child abuse. Legal aid, job referrals, help with welfare and housing, as well as other counseling and support are available.

The Fatherhood Project in Portland, Oregon tries to reach the male partners of teenage mothers and pregnant teenagers to offer ongoing support and referral services. The project attempts to involve fathers in the pregnancy and parenting process by running a group and providing peer support, parenting skill training, child development knowledge, counseling, role modeling, and encouragement of personal responsibility. The project links up young fathers with community resources so they can not only handle anxieties about being a father, but also become an asset in the childrearing process. One of the goals of the fatherhood project is to make a positive impact in the self-perception of young fathers and get them more involved in the care and nurturance of their child.

The Teen Fatherhood Project of Greater Bridgeport, Connecticut targets teen fathers and high-risk adolescent males in the Hispanic community. The

YMCA coordinates the project's activities through a variety of community agencies. Parenting classes, family life planning, and vocational training are among the offerings.

The Fatherhood Program in St. Paul provides parenting classes for young fathers and mothers and it emphasizes vocational skills training and job placement.

The Fathers' Outreach component of the Teen Parents' Program in Poughkeepsie, New York is conducted mostly through home visits in the community. Services for the young fathers include family planning, parenting classes, referral, and educational and vocational planning.

The Fatherhood Project in Louisville, Kentucky is an adjunct to the Teen-age Parent Program (TAPP) at Emerson School. TAPP serves approximately 400 girls annually and offers complete medical and social services as well as a full academic program for teenage mothers-to-be. The fatherhood project operates in the afternoon and evening hours and teen fathers benefit from training in prenatal and child care, advice on family planning, individual counseling, parenting classes, and educational and employment counseling. A Boy Scout vocational unit offers career counseling and job shadowing experiences for enrollment of the young fathers in job training programs.

Intergenerational Programs

An additional component of the Fatherhood Project in Louisville, Kentucky is the Grandparents Group. This group, composed of parents of project enrollees, attends classes to update child care techniques and participates in group sessions on communication skills to generate better understanding between parents and teens at what is often a difficult stage in the family's life. The grandparents are led by a family therapist.

One of the most innovative new programs combines the natural match of foster grandparents and teenage parents. Both older adults and teen parents are burgeoning populations whose combination makes for a perfect fit and the satisfaction of reciprocal needs. Older adults find meaningful ways of spending their time and teen fathers and mothers benefit from the guidance and help of proven experience.

In Wayne County, Michigan fifteen foster grandparents work in three teen parent programs (Walls 1987). Eligible students include pregnant teens and school-age mothers and fathers and their children. The major aim of the program is to provide comprehensive services so that boys and girls can stay in school and finish high school. Other health and counseling services, parenting classes, vocational training, child care services, and job preparation and placement are also available. The foster grandparents spend four-hour days with the children in the child care center—playing with the youngsters, feeding them, taking them for walks, and giving them lots of attention and love. Grandparents talk with the teen parents, listen to their problems, and lend a supportive ear. The teens pay attention to and respect the intergenerational views that they receive.

Legal Rights

The MALE (Maximizing a Life Experience) program in Decatur, Georgia was established to help teenage fathers understand their legal and emotional rights and responsibilities, identify present and future options, and obtain information about contraception. The nine-session program includes role playing sessions, films and group discussions on teen pregnancy, a speaker from Georgia's Legal Aid Society, and a field trip to Planned Parenthood.

Model Prevention Programs

Prevention programs target efforts to prevent teenagers from ever becoming parents in the first place. Their goals are more far reaching ones and often more controversial in nature. Facets of these programs include sex education in the early and later grades, open discussions and counseling regarding sexuality and human reproduction, contraception accessibility, and life planning.

Peer Programs and Role Models

The allure of the athlete and the power of positive role models are being used to combat teen pregnancy in Richmond, Virginia in a program called ACT 1 (Athletes Coaching Teens). Directed at teenage males, the program brings professional athletes to the schools to talk about teenage pregnancy to high school boys identified as athletic leaders in their schools. These high school leaders, in turn, pass the message of considering the consequences of unprotected intercourse and making good decisions where sex is concerned, to junior high boys. It is hoped that, in turn, the message of sexual responsibility filters down to the lower grades.

Project MARCH (Men Acting Responsibly for Contraception and Health) published a color poster of Bruce Arians, Temple Owls football coach, holding a football, pointing his finger, and saying, "Remember—a good defense is essential to winning in football. The same is true when it comes to preventing unplanned pregnancies and sexually transmitted diseases."

Another peer support program is Project Alpha, sponsored by the March of Dimes and Alpha Phi Alpha Fraternity in Chicago, Illinois. Project Alpha capitalizes on the success of black professional men—accountants, educators, psychologists, management consultants, administrators—and older boys who have excelled in sports or entertainment as a role model for preventing teenage fatherhood. Young teens are paired with older males who share the consequences of teenage pregnancy and a broader scope and goals for life decisions. A weekend conference on adolescent pregnancy is held where 100 black teen males from the Chicago area attend. The males are selected by social service agencies as leaders in their peer groups. They take part in discussions and hear talks on the male's role in adolescent pregnancy.

The Family Life Center Foundation in collaboration with the Shiloh Baptist Church in Washington, D.C. was awarded a grant from the Ford Foundation to establish a teen father prevention program. Black leaders from the Shiloh Men's Club informally adopt troubled youths in the neighborhood and spend time with them at the church's family life center (a multipurpose facility with basketball and racquetball courts, weight room, sauna, and jacuzzi), at sports events, or on field trips. Informal discussions or special meetings center on substance abuse, human sexuality, and the advantages of staying in school and preparing for a career.

Family Planning Programs

Efforts to involve teen males in family planning and teenage pregnancy prevention have been met with barriers at every turn. The federal funds that were set aside in the 1970s for male involvement in family planning were cut in the 1980s, and financial support for the male involvement component was extinguished. Evaluations of these programs also indicated that males underused the clinic services, making them not cost-effective (Casey & Cone 1986). Still, administrators of these programs and other advocates are convinced that there are enough males to benefit from these services to justify their continuation.

This problem is compounded to some extent by the fact that administrators of male involvement programs operate in a vacuum. They have few opportunities to share information with one another, there is practically no research literature to draw upon, and program evaluations on male involvement are almost nonexistent (Casey 1986). Progress towards eliminating these barriers was realized when the Center for Population Options held its first conference on male involvement in November of 1985. National and local representatives of family planning organizations convened to explore the state of male involvement and its future directions. The conference was followed by a newsletter, *Male Involvement Bulletin,* which published a series of articles on male involvement and family planning to help workers network and share and support their efforts.

Most of the family planning programs reported here were incorporated into an existing agency's service to young women, and most of them take a wholistic approach through health care and educational and vocational planning. The most innovative of these programs take their message into the streets. One of the most innovative of these outreach programs is the Young Men's Clinic at Columbia Presbyterian Hospital in New York, described at the beginning of this chapter.

Another community outreach program of this nature is the Male's Place in Charlotte, North Carolina, where males between the ages of 15 and 24 can get free medical examinations, sex counseling, and contraceptives. The clinic, housed in the County Health Department, also employs young men who go out to parts of the community where most teenage pregnancies occur and talk to boys about male sexual responsibilities, urge them to visit the clinic, and, when needed, distribute contraceptives.

The Young Men's Sexuality Awareness Program, sponsored by the Norfolk Area Health Education Center and financed by a one-year $1,600 grant from the State Department of Mental Health and Mental Retardation, began in October 1986.* As necessary as this program is and with its inherent possibilities, it is one of only a handful in the area to follow a national trend of targeting teenage boys for sex education.

The aim is not to get teenagers to say "no" to sex. Program leaders think that is not a realistic goal. The program, instead, is designed to teach the youngsters responsibility and to make them think about their values and self-respect.

The eight-week course is free and open to young men age 14 through 18. The classes are held once every two weeks at two sites outside of the schools. The Health Education Center, affiliated with Eastern Virginia Medical School, plans to bring the program to other neighborhoods. It has applied for a two-year federal grant to conduct classes at four Norfolk sites.

Participants learn about topics ranging from sexuality, birth control, and sexually transmitted diseases, to fatherhood, child care, and preparing for childbirth. Frederick I. Watson, leader of the program, believes that it is just as important, if not more so, to train males as well as females in sex education—males could produce a child every day of the month, whereas women are able to conceive only once a month.

Local experts in dealing with teenage pregnancy in Norfolk say programs for boys are needed if the cause of teenage pregnancy—and not just the symptom, the pregnant girls themselves—is to be treated. The youthful males say they like the program and see a need for it. They need somewhere to go to get answers to their questions.

The Young Males Pilot Project in California is a preventive program

---

*The following description of this program is reprinted from *Prevention & Promotion Bulletin,* January 1987. Department of Mental Health, Mental Retardation, and Substance Abuse. Office of Prevention, Promotion, and Library Services, Richmond, Virginia.

aimed at black, Hispanic, Asian, and Native American youth (Johnson & Staples 1979). This program provides information on family life education, family planning, and parental concern with the goal of developing sexual responsibility and reducing repeated and unwanted out-of-wedlock pregnancies through goal-directed support and assistance to young and unwed fathers between the ages of 14 and 24.

Project MARCH (Men Acting Responsibly for Contraception and Health) is a combined health clinic and community education program for young men in Philadelphia. Aggressive outreach advertising in Philadelphia's mass transit system has informed citizens of the clinic's services. Mottos such as "Real Men Don't Become Fathers Before They Are Ready" and "Real Men Do Use Condoms" emblazon the project's literature. As one of the few educational outreach programs specifically designed for young men, Project MARCH provides reliable information about sex and the male role in reproductive health. The project coordinator leads "man-to-man" rap sessions free to any interested school, church group, or other community organization that serves young men between 13 and 21 years of age. Through small group discussions, lectures, films, and exercises, young men confront such pressing issues as sound decision making in regard to sex and contraception, becoming a father, and male and female reproductive physiology. Topics such as "Growing up Male," "Giving Guys a Choice," or "Teen Pregnancy from the Male Viewpoint" are examples of the various workshops that are conducted.

The Male Adolescent Program is housed at Rush-Presbyterian-St. Lukes Medical Center in Chicago, Illinois. Among the many outreach program topics are sexually transmitted diseases, contraception, pregnancy and childbirth, and interpersonal relationships. The program aims to teach teenage males the consequences of fatherhood, contraceptive information, and how to prepare for the role of fatherhood for those who have already fathered a child.

School-Based Health Clinics

The comprehensive school-based health clinic movement is the most recent approach in preventing adolescent pregnancy. Through a grass-roots movement, school-based health clinics are growing by leaps and bounds. Sharon Lovick (1987), the nation's leading authority on school-based health clinics, reported that with their wholistic approach to health, school clinics are the wave of the future. At the beginning of 1987, a total of seventy-six sites existed and eight were in the process of being established. Projections were that by 1989 an additional 200 sites would be in operation, aided by a national resource designed to assist current and emerging sites and sponsored by the Center for Population Options (see chapter 9 for program names and addresses).

The clinics, although located on junior and senior high school grounds, are staffed by nurses and physicians, and administered by such outside organizations as departments of public health, medical schools, or community health centers. School-based health clinics are unique in their concern with the overall physical and emotional health of teenagers (Kirby 1986). Among the comprehensive services provided are athletic physical examinations; general health assessments; screenings for sexually transmitted diseases and other illnesses; immunizations; dental hygiene; first aid and health; family planning counseling; sex education; prenatal and postpartum care; nutrition and weight control programs; substance abuse programs; and referrals for special medical care. Some clinics either offer contraceptive prescriptions on site or refer students to off-site birth control clinics (Dryfoos 1985).

Despite the fact that the major goal is primary health care, school-based health clinics are steeped in controversy because a small part of their services entail the dispensation of birth control. In the minds of critics, the school-based programs are "sex clinics"—places where teenagers are handed contraceptives and sent on their merry way. The truth is, however, that they were never designed as such and that only 26 percent of them provide contraception. Those that do offer birth control pills and condoms do so only with parental consent, and none of the programs perform abortions (Lovick 1987). Less than 25 percent of the programs have anything to do with sexuality or reproduction.

Regardless of the controversy, data indicate that the clinics are being widely used by males and females equally. A clinic in Chicago recorded over two thousand medical encounters after only two months of operation, and 70 percent of students in Kansas City, 75 percent in St. Paul, and 85 percent in Dallas take advantage of the clinic's services (Kirby 1986).

The first public high school to house a health clinic was established by the St. Paul-Ramsey Medical Center in 1973. The clinic offered immunizations, treatment for sexually transmitted diseases, and physical examinations for athletes. It provided contraception counseling and dispensed prescriptions for birth control. Most school-based clinics are modeled on the St. Paul program.

The Fifth Ward Enrichment Program in Houston, Texas is a school-based clinic, especially for boys between the ages of 11 and 13. Physical exams, sex education, discussions and dispensation of contraception are part of a broad-based approach that also includes academic tutoring and a life option focus, involving decision making, interpersonal communication, and other life management skills. During after-school hours, recreational activities such as chess, martial arts, drama, organized sports, business education, life skills, and problem-solving groups are offered. Monthly field trips are also taken, and parents are urged to participate as much as possible. The program is a two-year one that begins when boys are still in middle school. Most of the boys are from mother-headed families and the program staff function as teacher, friend, big brother, and favorite uncle and father (Adams 1987).

Life Options Approach

There is wide agreement among experts that family planning, contraceptive counseling, and health clinic services are only part and parcel of the whole prevention package. Although programs must impress upon teenagers the advantages of postponing sexual activity, saying "no" to sex will not stick when adolescents are faced with poverty, low self-esteem, and lack of a future on the horizon. Teens cannot make decisions from a moral framework when their daily interactions are outside that framework (Lovick 1987). There is growing recognition among professionals that programs should give teenagers a sense that their life choices will be severely limited by becoming parents. Major funding agencies such as the Ford Foundation and advocacy groups like the Children's Defense Fund and the Center for Population Options have developed literature, media, and programs that target this broad-based perspective.

The Children's Defense Fund (CDF) believes that youth with hope and positive life options are more likely to delay early parenting (Pittman & Govan 1986). CDF has wholeheartedly endorsed such a broad-based approach to adolescent pregnancy prevention, for as the organization acknowledges, feelings of self-esteem and "Who am I?" are strongly connected with decisions about contraception and sexuality. CDF operates on the assumption that adolescents with clear goals for their lives and with strong achievement motivation are less likely to become sexually active at younger ages and more likely, if sexually active, to be regular and effective contraceptive users.

CDF's priorities reflect today's emphasis on prevention rather than intervention. Their first goal is to prevent an adolescent's first pregnancy, their second goal is to prevent repeat pregnancies, and their third goal is to ensure the welfare and care of babies born to adolescent parents. CDF advocates for programs that offer teens better educational and career choices and more experience in self-sufficiency and responsible decision making. CDF's fifteen-point plan calls on federal, state, and local governments to provide more comprehensive sex education in schools early, before children become sexually active and in a context where responsible decision making is strengthened. It further recommends establishing or strengthening vocational scholarships, community learning centers, job creation, school drop-out prevention, adolescent health care, and after-school programs for 10- to 15-year-olds (Meyer & Russell 1986).

The Center for Population Options (CPO) has developed a curriculum integrating sexuality and employment education, called *Life Planning Education*. The curriculum deals with self-esteem, personal and family values, goal setting and decision making, and parenthood, sexuality, employment, and communication. In parts of the country where the curriculum has been implemented, teens showed increases in knowledge about sexuality, in the number of kinds of jobs they thought they could have, and in the number of things they wanted to do or acquire before they become parents. The CPO has published an excellent workbook, called *Make a Life for Yourself,* containing questions which teens can read and respond to that stimulate thought about their future life goals (see chapter 9 for more information on where to write and other resources of this nature).

New York City's Junior High School 54 in West Side Manhattan is an example of an after-school education and recreation program that offers boys and girls an array of activities from which to choose. Program participants receive a blend of help with homework, health and sex education, and remedial tutoring, combined with competitive sports and other recreational activities. An outside agency provides mental health counseling and leadership training (Pittman & Govan 1986). Most other after-school programs fit the life options model in the sense that they offer wholistic approaches for school-age youngsters. For a more detailed discussion of these after-school programs, see Robinson, Rowland, and Coleman (1986). For further reading on intervention and prevention programs for teenage fathers, the following resources are suggested:

Casey, S., & Cone, S.E. (1986) *Programs at a glance.* Washington, D.C.: Center for Population Options.

Klinman, D., & Kohl, R. (1984) *Fatherhood U.S.A.* New York: Garland Press.

Nickel, P.S., & Delany, H. (1985) *Working with teen parents: A survey of promising approaches.* Chicago: Family Focus and Family Resource Coalition.

Pittman, K., & Govan, C. (1986) *Model programs: Preventing adolescent pregnancy and building youth self-sufficiency.* Washington, D.C.: Children's Defense Fund Adolescent Pregnancy Prevention Clearinghouse.

Evaluation of Adolescent Pregnancy Programs

Evaluations of pregnancy prevention programs have fallen behind the initiation of programs. In general there have been few attempts to evaluate the efficacy of teen pregnancy programs. Many sound programs are more interested in providing services rather than involving themselves in the time-consuming business of collecting data, analyzing it, and writing the results for public consumption. Where evaluative attempts have been made, outcomes are inconclusive or highly questionable. An assessment of ten intervention adolescent mother programs in four states indicated that program advocates and service providers set overly ambitious goals for short intervention periods and exaggerated the potential benefits of services in order to secure political and national support (Weatherley et al. 1986). A fundamental question, the researchers claimed, was whether the comprehensive model could actually produce the results sought by its supporters.

Many outcomes remain unclear because of conflicting reports, especially where programs are controversial. Opponents of sex education, for example, claim that it increases the likelihood of sexual activity and pregnancy among adolescents; proponents say that it has no such effect, and in fact, reduces the rate of pregnancy by promoting more effective contraceptive practice (Marsiglio & Mott 1986).

Evaluation of prevention programs is difficult because of the controversy surrounding sex education programs and school-based health clinics that often makes legitimate assessments difficult or impossible. Probing into the lives of adolescents, for instance, to determine their sexual behaviors can raise resistance from many areas. In addition, the inconsistency of program content and the researcher's definition of sex education from one study to the next have led to ambiguous results. Improper methodological procedures by schools and agencies have defaced the credibility of evaluation outcomes, and longitudinal studies that have been conducted lack generalizability to all parts of the nation.

Evaluation of Intervention Programs

Generally, there have been few attempts to evaluate the efficacy of parenting programs for teen parents. One of the few exceptions is the Teen Father Collaboration Project, administered by the Bank Street College of Education. The program offered vocational assistance, counseling, and classes in prenatal development and parenting. Four hundred teenage fathers participated, and at the end of two years an evaluation of the program was made in eight U.S. cities. Results showed that 82 percent of the boys had daily contact with their children; 74 percent provided financial support; and 90 percent still had relationships with the mothers of their babies (Stengel 1985). Moreover, 61 percent of the young men who had been out of work found jobs, and 46 percent of those who had dropped out of school had resumed their education.

Another study measured parenting skills of thirty-one teenage mothers, recruited from three urban parenting programs in Arizona (Roosa 1984).

Pretests on child development knowledge, human reproduction, and parenting attitudes were administered in January and identical posttests were administered again in May. Results indicated a significant improvement in knowledge of child development and human reproduction. Parenting attitudes, in contrast, showed no change during the four-month period.

These findings suggested that, although teen parents may learn appropriate developmental information for their children, their attitudes may preclude putting this knowledge into practice with any consistency. So intervention programs should help adolescent parents recognize and accept responsibility for their offspring in addition to teaching facts on child development. Where adolescent sexual behavior is concerned, sheer knowledge is not an assurance that responsible sexual behavior will occur. Programs should couple the emphasis on simply disseminating correct information on reproductive physiology with helping teens acknowledge their sexuality, learn decision-making skills, and improve methods of communicating decisions about sexual behavior so that they can be more responsible in their sexual behavior.

Evaluation of Prevention Programs

Research on a handful of adolescents (seven males and twelve females) between the ages of 14 and 18 suggests that programs that teach adolescent decision making and interpersonal skills are effective in pregnancy prevention (Blythe, Gilchrist & Schinke 1981). One group of these adolescents received instruction on human sexuality and training in decision making and interpersonal skills. Leaders of the program helped participants apply the information in planning and evaluating the consequences of future actions. A control group of teens received no instruction of any kind. Results indicated the groups receiving instruction to be significantly more knowledgeable about human sexuality, better decision makers, and more skillful at interpersonal communication. A three- to six-month follow-up revealed teenagers who participated in group sessions were more committed to postponing pregnancy, used birth control more frequently, and had relied more often on more effective methods of birth control than did nonparticipants.

Other data confirm that sex education programs per se have no bearing on whether or not teenagers engage in sexual intercourse. Sex education does, however, increase the likelihood that sexually active teens have better contraceptive knowledge and are more likely to practice contraception than adolescents not receiving instruction (Dawson 1986).

Older sexually active girls who have previously had a sex education course are significantly more likely to use an effective contraceptive method than are those who have never taken a course (Marsiglio & Mott 1986). The researchers also concluded that, "This relationship may offset any effect that a sex education course may have in raising the likelihood of early first coitus, since no significant association can be found between taking a sex education course and subsequently becoming premaritally pregnant before age 20" (p. 151).

School-Based Health Clinics

The wholistic approach of school-based health clinics seems to be highly effective in reducing adolescent pregnancy. Where school-based clinics were used between 1977 and 1984, births to female students fell from 59 per thousand to 26 per thousand, and the drop-out rate in one high school fell from 45 percent to 10 percent (Wallis 1985). Evaluation reports from school-based health clinics in Muskegan, Michigan and Dallas, Texas also show declines in teenage birthrates since the clinics opened their doors (Dryfoos 1985). Teenage clinic patients in the West Dallas Youth Clinic had lower birthrates than their contemporaries who did not take advantage of the clinic's services (Ralph & Edgington 1983). Fully 80 percent of the adolescent mothers in the St. Paul program remained in school after childbirth and of this number fewer had repeat pregnancies than those who dropped out of school (Zellman 1982). Program administrators in other areas attribute improved school attendance and lower drop-out rates to school-based clinics, although further research confirmation of these claims is needed (Dryfoos 1985).

With all of their benefits, school-based clinics are not without their problems. Despite their major advantages of comprehensiveness, researchers found at least four obstacles to school-based programs in ten sites (Weatherley et al. 1986). Losses of financial support and budget cuts led to financial constraints. There were limited services from community agencies in local sites and barriers to providing services in those areas. Political competition with other worthy causes limited resources, and condemnatory public views of adolescent pregnancy as well as claims that service advocates were promoting rather than circumventing unwanted pregnancies made school-based clinics an unpopular cause. Last and perhaps most severe, there remained unconvincing proof of program outcomes.

Still, strong evidence in support of school-based health clinics is hard to ignore. The most convincing report resulted from a collaboration program between The Johns Hopkins School of Medicine and school-based health clinics in the Baltimore School System (Zabin et al. 1986). The project provided students attending one of the junior high schools and one of the senior high schools with sexuality and contraception education, individual and group counseling, and medical and contraceptive services for approximately three years. Students in the remaining two schools received no such services and served as the control group.

Statistically significant changes occurred over the course of two and a half years in sexual and contraceptive knowledge. One of the most striking findings was that boys in junior high used the clinic equally as often as their female agemates. Pregnancy rates were reduced by as much as 30 percent and first-time sexual intercourse among junior and senior high students showed sharp delays by as much as seven months. Those boys and girls who did engage in sexual activity and who had received the program's benefits, were more likely to seek birth control before their first sexual encounter. In schools that did not have the program, however, there was a 58 percent increase in pregnancies during the course of the investigation.

Conclusion

Although few in number, the growth of programs designed exclusively to assist teenage fathers offers hope in arresting the cycle of children producing children. Programs such as these also go a long way toward helping those young men who are fathers to become more competent in their roles and toward preventing repeat pregnancies. Although these programs are promising, additional preventive programs on family planning and responsibilities of parenthood are needed to reduce the numbers of adolescent fathers.

Future programs must continue to include the teenage father and have both a preventive and remedial emphasis. More innovative programs are needed whereby social agencies take more assertive measures to serve young fathers. Current evidence suggests that of those who complete a program, the majority turn out to be responsible and caring parents. One young man who completed the Teen Pregnancy and Parenting Project in San Francisco is now a counselor there. A product of teenage parents and a teen father of a 17-month-old, he is convinced the experience helped break the cycle: "My father was a parent when he was a teenager. My mother and grandmother were. It didn't stop with me or with my brothers. I know it will stop with my son." (Stengel 1985, p. 90).

In its sobering report, *Teenage Pregnancy: The Problem That Hasn't Gone Away,* the Alan Guttmacher Institute (1982) concluded that, "Teenage pregnancy—the problem that nobody wants—has not gone away. Nor will it unless there is heightened awareness and commitment and a willingness to abandon simplistic approaches, to take bold and often controversial steps, and to pay the necessary price."

References

Adams, M.L. (1987) *Fifth ward enrichment program evaluation report: 1985–1986.* Houston, Texas: Fifth Ward Enrichment Program.

Alan Guttmacher Institute. (1982) *Teenage pregnancy: The problem that hasn't gone away.* New York: Alan Guttmacher Institute.

Allen-Meares, P. (1984) Adolescent pregnancy and parenting: The forgotten adolescent father and his parents. *Journal of Social Work & Human Sexuality* 3:27–38.

Blythe, B.J., Gilchrist, L.D., & Schinke, S.P. (1981) Pregnancy-prevention groups for adolescents. *Social Work* 26:503–504.

Bolton, F. (1980) *The pregnant adolescent: Problems of premature parenthood.* Beverly Hills, Ca.: Sage.

Brown, S.V. (1983) The commitment and concerns of black adolescent parents. *Social Work Research & Abstracts* 19:27–34.

Casey, S. (1986) The missing ingredient: Involving young men in family planning. *Male Involvement Bulletin* (May): 1–5.

Casey, S., & Cone, S.E. (1986) *Programs at a glance.* Washington, D.C.: Center for Population Options.

Dawson, D.A. (1986) The effects of sex education on adolescent behavior. *Family Planning Perspectives* 18:162–65.

Dryfoos, J. (1985) School-based health clinics: A new approach to preventing adolescent pregnancy? *Family Planning Perspectives* 17:70–75.

Earls, F., & Siegel, B. (1980) Precocious fathers. *American Journal of Orthopsychiatry* 50:469–80.

Elster, A.B., & Panzarine, S. (1979) Adolescent pregnancy—Where is the teenage father? *Pediatrics* 63:824.

Furstenberg, F. (1976) *Unplanned parenthood: The social consequences of teenage childbearing.* New York: The Free Press.

Furstenberg, F., Brooks-Gunn, J., & Morgan, S.P. (1987) *Adolescent mothers in later life.* New York: Cambridge University Press.

Goldstein, H., & Wallace, H.M. (1978) Services for and needs of pregnant teenagers in large cities of the United States, 1976. *Public Health Reports* 93:46–54.

Johnson, L.B., & Staples, R.E. (1979) Family planning and the young minority male: A pilot project. *The Family Coordinator* 28:535–43.

Kirby, D. (1986) Comprehensive school-based health clinics: A growing movement to improve adolescent health and reduce teenage pregnancy. *Journal of School Health* 56:289–91.

Klinman, D. (1984) *Fatherhood U.S.A.* New York: Garland Press.

Knowles, G.A., & Tripple, P.A. (1986) Cyesis program addresses teenage pregnancy and family well-being. *Journal of Home Economics* 51:25–28.

Lovick, S. (5 February 1987) Uniting the links in prevention. Speech presented at the Annual Meeting of the Council on Adolescent Pregnancy, Charlotte, North Carolina.

Marsiglio, W., & Mott, F.L. (1986) The impact of sex education on sexual activity, contraceptive use and premarital pregnancy among American teenagers. *Family Planning Perspectives* 18:151–61.

Meyer, P., & Russell, A. (1986) Adolescent pregnancy: Testing prevention strategies. *Carnegie Quarterly* 31:1–8.

Pierce, A.D. (1981) Adoption policy and the "unwed father"; An exploratory study of social worker response to changing conceptions of fatherhood. *Dissertation Abstracts International* 42:387-A.

Pittman, K., & Govan, C. (1986) *Model programs: Preventing adolescent pregnancy and building youth self-sufficiency.* Washington, D.C.: Children's Defense Fund Adolescent Pregnancy Prevention Clearinghouse.

Ralph, N., & Edgington, E. (1983) An evaluation of an adolescent family planning program. *Journal of Adolescent Health Care* 4:158.

Robinson, B.E., Rowland, B.H., & Coleman, M. (1986) *Latchkey kids: Unlocking doors for children and their families.* Lexington, Mass.: Lexington Books.

Roosa, M. (1984) Short-term effects of teenage parenting programs on knowledge and attitudes. *Adolescence* 19:659–66.

Stengel, R. (9 December 1985) The missing father myth. *Time:*90.

Wallis, C. (9 December 1985) Children having children. *Time:*78–90.

Walls, N. (1987) Three generations of love. *Children Today* (April): 2–5.

Washington, A.C., & Rosser, P.L. (25 August 1981) A comparison of three approaches to psychosocial services for teenage parents. Paper presented at the 89th Annual Convention of the American Psychological Association, Los Angeles, California.

Weatherly, R.A., Perlman, S.B., Levine, M.H., & Klerman, L.V. (1986) Comprehensive programs for pregnant teenagers and teenage parents: How successful have they been? *Family Planning Perspectives,* 18:73–78.

Zabin, L.S., Hirsch, M.B., Smith, E.A., Street, R., & Hardy, J.B. (1986) Evaluation of a pregnancy prevention program for urban teenagers. *Family Planning Perspectives* 18:119–26.

Zellman, G.I. (1982) Public school programs for adolescent pregnancy and parenthood: An assessment. *Family Planning Perspectives,* 14:15.

9
Resources on Teenage Fathers

This chapter contains annotations of books for adults and children, organizations, periodicals, audiovisuals, unpublished research reports, model programs, and publications for researchers, program developers, parents, teachers, and other human service workers—all pertaining to teenage fatherhood and adolescent pregnancy.

Books for Adults

Teenage Sexuality, Pregnancy, and Childbearing

Alan Guttmacher Institute. (1982) *Teenage pregnancy: The problem that hasn't gone away.* New York: Alan Guttmacher Institute.

Allen, J.E. (1980) *Managing teenage pregnancy: Access to abortion, contraception, and sex education.* New York: Praeger.

Bolton, F. (1983) *The pregnant adolescent.* Beverly Hills, Ca.: Sage.

Byrne, D., & Fisher, W.A. (1985) *Adolescents, sex, and contraception.* Hillsdale, New Jersey: Lawrence Erlbaum.

Chilman, C.S. (1983) *Adolescent sexuality in a changing American society.* New York: Wiley.

Frank, D.B. (1983) *Deep blue funk & other stories: Portraits of teenage parents.* Chicago: The Ounce of Prevention Fund.

Furstenberg, F.F. (1976) *Unplanned parenthood: The social consequences of teenage childbearing.* New York: The Free Press.

Furstenberg, F.F., Brooks-Gunn, J., & Morgan, S.P. (1987) *Adolescent mothers in later life.* Cambridge: Cambridge University Press.

Furstenberg, F.F., Lincoln, R., & Menken, J. (eds.) (1980) *Perspective on teenage sexuality, pregnancy, and childbearing.* Philadelphia: University of Pennsylvania Press.

Haggstrom, G.W., Blaschke, T.J., Kanouse, D.E., Lisowski, W., & Morrison, P.A. (1981) *Teenage parents: Their ambitions and attainments.* Santa Monica, Ca.: Rand Corporation.

Lewis, H.R., & Lewis, M.E. (1982) *The parent's guide to teenage sex and pregnancy.* New York: Berkley/Jove Publishing Group.

Moore, K.A., & Burt, M.R. (1982) *Private crisis, public cost: Policy perspectives on teenage childbearing.* Washington, D.C.: Urban Institute Press.

Nickel, P.S., & Delany, H. (1985) *Working with teen parents: A survey of promising approaches.* Chicago: Family Resource Coalition.

Nye, F.I., & Lamberts, M.B. (1980) *School-age parenthood: Consequences for babies, mothers, fathers, grandparents, and others.* Cooperative Extension Bulletin 0667. Pullman: Washington State University.

Ooms, T. (Ed.) (1981) *Teenage pregnancy in a family context: Implications for policy.* Philadelphia: Temple University Press.

Roggow, L., & Owens, C. (1984) *Handbook for pregnant teenagers.* Grand Rapids, Minn.: Zondervan.

Scott, K., Field, T., & Robertson, E. (eds.) (1980) *Teenage parents and their offspring.* New York: Grune & Stratton.

Shapiro, C. (1981) *Adolescent pregnancy prevention: School-community cooperation.* Springfield, Illinois: Charles C. Thomas.

Smith, P.B., & Mumford, D.M. (eds.) (1980) *Adolescent pregnancy: Perspectives for the health professional.* Boston: G.K. Hall.

Sorenson, R. (1973) *Adolescent sexuality in contemporary America.* New York: World Publishing Company.

Stuart, I.R., & Wells, C.F. (1981) *Pregnancy in adolescence.* New York: Van Nostrand Reinhold.

Zelnik, M., Kanter, J., & Ford, K. (1981) *Sex and pregnancy in adolescence.* Beverly Hills, Ca.: Sage

Teenage Fatherhood

Anastasiow, N., Anastasiow, M., & Carlson, C. (1982) *The adolescent parent.* Baltimore: Brookes Publishing Company.

Barret, R.L., & Robinson, B.E. (1985) "The adolescent father." In S. Hanson & F. Bozett (eds.), *Dimensions of fatherhood,* pp. 353–68. Beverly Hills, Ca.: Sage.

Barret, R.L. & Robinson, B.E. (1987) "The role of adolescent fathers in parenting and childrearing." In A.R. Stiffman & R.A. Feldman (eds.), *Advances in adolescent mental health.* Vol. IV, *Childbearing and childrearing.* Greenwich, Conn.: JAI Press.

Barret, R.L., & Robinson, B.E. (1987) "Teenage fathers: Neglected too long." *Hot topics series: Teenage pregnancy.* Bloomington, Indiana: Phi Delta Kappa.

Battle, S.F. (1987) *The black adolescent parent.* New York: The Haworth Press.

Bode, J. (1980) *Kids having kids: The unwed teenage parent.* New York: Watts, Franklin.

Elster, A.B., & Lamb, M.E. (eds.) (1986) *Adolescent fatherhood.* Hillsdale, New Jersey: Lawrence Erlbaum.

Elster, A.B., & Lamb, M.E. (1987) "Adolescent fathers: The understudied side of adolescent pregnancy." In J.B. Lancaster & B.A. Hamburg (eds.), *School-aged pregnancy and parenthood: Biosocial dimensions.* Chicago: Aldine.

Elster, A.B., & Panzarine, S.L. (1983) "Adolescent fathers." In E.R. McAnarney (ed.), *Premature adolescent pregnancy and parenthood,* pp. 231–52. New York: Grune & Stratton.

Herzog, J.M. (1984) "Boys who make babies." In M. Sugar (ed.), *Adolescent parenthood.* New York: Spectrum Publications.

Jensen, L., & Kingston, M. (1986) *Parenting.* New York: CBS.

Klinman, D., & Kohl, R. (1984) *Fatherhood USA.* New York: Garland.

Klinman, D., & Sander, J. (1985) *Reaching and serving the teenage father.* New York: Bank Street College of Education.

Levering, C., & Duncket, J. (1982) *Teenage pregnancy and parenthood.* New York: The Association of Junior Leagues.

McAnarney, E.R. (1982) *Premature adolescent pregnancy and parenthood.* New York: Grune & Stratton.

McAnarney, E.R., & Stickle, G. (1981) *Pregnancy and childbearing during adolescence: Research priorities for the 1980s.* New York: Alan R. Liss.

Pannor, R., Massarik, F., & Evans, B. (1971) *The unmarried father: New helping approaches for unmarried young parents.* New York: Springer.

Robinson, B.E., & Barret, R.L. (1986) "Teenage fathers." In *The developing father.* New York: The Guilford Press.

Ross, A. (1982) *Teenage mothers, teenage fathers.* New York: Everest House.

Adolescent Growth and Development

Conger, J.J., & Peterson, A.C. (1984) *Adolescence and youth: Psychological development in a changing world.* 3rd ed. New York: Harper & Row.

Flake-Hobson, C., Robinson, B.E., & Skeen, P. (1983) *Child development and relationships.* New York: Random House.

Fuhrmann, B.S. (1986) *Adolescence, adolescents.* Boston: Little, Brown and Company.

Kimmel, D.C., & Weiner, I.B. (1985) *Adolescence: A developmental transition.* Hillsdale, New Jersey: Lawrence Erlbaum.

Leigh, G.K., & Peterson, G.W. (1986) *Adolescents in families.* Cincinnati, Ohio: South-Western Publishing Company.

Lloyd, M.A. (1985) *Adolescence.* New York: Harper and Row.

McKinney, J.P., Fitzgerald, H.E., & Strommen, E.A. (1982) *Developmental psychology: The adolescent and young adult.* Homewood, Illinois: The Dorsey Press.

Newman, B.M., & Newman, P.R. (1986) *Adolescent development.* Columbus, Ohio: Merrill Publishing Company.

Offer, D., Ostrov, E., & Howard, K.I. (1984) *Patterns of adolescent self-image.* San Francisco: Jossey-Bass, Inc.

Rice, F.P. (1981) *The adolescent: Development, relationships, and culture.* 3d ed. Boston: Allyn & Bacon.

Robinson, B.E., Rowland, B.H., & Coleman, M. (1986) *Latchkey kids: Unlocking doors for children and their families.* Lexington, Mass.: Lexington Books.

Santrock, J.W. (1984) *Adolescence.* 2d ed. Dubuque, Iowa: William C. Brown.

Santrock, J.W., & Yussen, S.R. (1984) *Children and adolescents: A developmental perspective.* Dubuque, Iowa: William C. Brown.

Seltzer, V.C. (1982) *Adolescent social development: Dynamic functional interaction.* Lexington, Mass.: Lexington Books.

Stevens-Long, J., & Cobb, M.J. (1983) *Adolescence and early adulthood.* Palo Alto, Ca.: Mayfield.

Zigler, E., & Stevenson, M. (1987) *Children: Development and social issues.* Lexington, Mass.: D.C. Heath & Company.

Books for Adolescents and Children

Haffner, D. & Casey, S. *Make a life for yourself.* Washington, D.C.: Center for Population Options. A booklet for teens about life planning. Deals with planning for education, career, and waiting to have babies.

Lindsay, J.W. *Do I have a daddy?* Buena Park, Ca.: Morning Glory Press. A story about a single-parent child. Gives sensible advice about what to tell children and how to tell them. (Early childhood.)

Lindsay, J.W. *Teens parenting: The challenge of babies and toddlers.* Buena Park, Ca.: Morning Glory Press. This book explores what it's really like to parent a child while you're still in school. (Sixth-grade reading level.)

Lindsay, J.W. *Teenage marriage: Coping with reality.* Buena Park, Ca.: Morning Glory Press. Gives teenagers a picture of the realities of marriage—a look at the difficulties they may encounter if they say "I do," or simply move in together, too soon. (Sixth-grade reading level.)

Lindsay, J.W. *Teens look at marriage: Rainbows, roles and reality.* Buena Park, Ca.: Morning Glory Press. Includes statistical information about teenagers' attitudes toward marriage and living together. Attitudes of teens not yet married are compared with those who are.

Lindsay, J.W. *Pregnant too soon: Adoption is an option.* Buena Park, Ca.: Morning Glory Press. Young women who were, by their own admission, "pregnant too soon," tell their stories. Most made the unpopular decision to release for adoption. Latest information on agency and independent adoption, fathers' rights, dealing with grief, and other aspects of adoption. (Fifth-grade reading level.)

Roggow, L., and C. Owens. *Handbook for pregnant teenagers.* Grand

Rapids, Minn.: Zondervan. Teenagers are taken step by step through the experiences and decisions of the pregnancy.

Special Reports

Alan Guttmacher Institute. (1981) *Factbook on teenage pregnancy.* New York: Alan Guttmacher Institute.

Alan Guttmacher Institute. (1981) *Teenage pregnancy: The problem that hasn't gone away.* New York: Alan Guttmacher Institute.

Alan Guttmacher Institute. (1981) *Teenage sexuality, pregnancy, and childbearing.* New York: Alan Guttmacher Institute.

Children's Defense Fund. (1985) *Black and white children in America: Key facts.* Washington, D.C.: Adolescent Pregnancy Prevention Clearinghouse.

Children's Defense Fund. (1985) *Preventing children having children.* Washington, D.C.: Adolescent Pregnancy Prevention Clearinghouse.

Children's Defense Fund. (1986) *Adolescent pregnancy: What the states are saying.* Washington, D.C.: Adolescent Pregnancy Prevention Clearinghouse.

Children's Defense Fund. (1986) *Adolescent pregnancy: Whose problem is it?* Washington, D.C.: Adolescent Pregnancy Prevention Clearinghouse.

Children's Defense Fund. (1986) *Building health programs for teenagers.* Washington, D.C.: Adolescent Pregnancy Prevention Clearinghouse.

Children's Defense Fund. (1986) *Maternal and child health data book: The health of America's children.* Washington, D.C.: Adolescent Pregnancy Prevention Clearinghouse.

Children's Defense Fund. (1986) *Model programs: Preventing adolescent pregnancy and building youth self-sufficiency.* Washington, D.C.: Adolescent Pregnancy Prevention Clearinghouse.

Group for the Advancement of Psychiatry. (1986) *Teenage pregnancy: Impact on adolescent development.* New York: Brunner/Mazel.

National Council on Family Relations. (1986) *Teenage pregnancy: An annotated bibliography.* St. Paul, Minn.: Family Resources Database.

National Research Council. (1987) *Risking the future, adolescent sexu-

ality, pregnancy, and childbearing. National Research Council: National Academy Press.

Organizations

This section details the major organizations concerned with school-age pregnancy and teenage fathers. The organizations have been divided into two types: resource organizations and professional organizations. Resource organizations provide such services as dissemination of information on adolescent sexuality, contraception, and pregnancy; replication models for teenage parenting programs; and other types of technical assistance in the area of teenage parenthood. Professional organizations are national associations of professionals dedicated to the improvement of those who work with adolescents. These organizations generally charge membership dues, publish journals, and sponsor an annual meeting where members gather for seminars, speeches, and workshops.

Resource Organizations

Academy for Educational Development. 1255 23rd Street, N.W., Washington, D.C. 20037. Serves the educational, social, health, and cultural needs of society by identifying and solving problems. With private foundation funds, the AED is involving middle schools and community agencies in pregnancy prevention efforts in eight urban school districts nationwide.

Adolescent Pregnancy Prevention Clearinghouse. Children's Defense Fund, 122 C Street, N.W., Washington, D.C. 20001. Under the auspices of the Children's Defense Fund, the clearinghouse publishes six reports a year on preventing children having children.

Alan Guttmacher Institute. 360 Park Avenue, New York, New York 10010. This is a tax-exempt nonprofit organization that conducts projects in the areas of research, policy analysis, and public education—all related to childbirth and family planning.

Center for Early Adolescence. Suite 223, Car Mill Mall, Carroboro, North Carolina 27510. As part of the Department of Maternal and Child Health at the University of North Carolina at Chapel Hill, the center disseminates information such as resource lists and bibliographies that deal with school-age children and adolescents. The center's quarterly newsletter is filled with valuable resources such as programs, research,

books, films, and conferences for professionals who work with teenagers.

Center for Population Options. 1012 14th Street, N.W., Suite 1200,
Washington, D.C. 20005. Works to enhance opportunities for young
people in key decision areas of their lives: continuing their education,
planning their families, obtaining needed health and social services, and
attaining productive employment. Special emphasis on interconnections
between family formation and other life actions.

Children's Defense Fund. 122 C Street, N.W., Washington, D.C. 20001.
Monitors programs addressing the health, educational, and nutritional
needs of children. Launched a special media campaign on teen pregnancy
prevention that counters the attitude that engaging in sex is without consequence.

Family Resource Coalition. 230 North Michigan Avenue, Suite 1625,
Chicago, Illinois 60601. Attempts to improve the content and expand
the number of programs available to parents. A preventive approach as-
sists families before their needs become acute and costly. Teenage parenthood prevention and working with teen parents is a special focus of this
group.

Family Resources Database. National Council on Family Relations. 1910
West County Road B, Suite 147, St. Paul, Minnesota 55113. A comput-
erized core collection of literature, programs, directories, and services of
the family and allied fields. Teenage pregnancy is one of its 130 subject
areas included in the database.

The Fatherhood Project. Bank Street College, 610 West 112 Street, New
York, New York 10025. This project, supported by private foundations,
encourages the development of new options for male involvement in
childrearing. The project operates a national clearinghouse for information about men in various fathering roles, including teenage fathers.

National Clearinghouse for Family Planning Information. P.O. Box
2225, Rockville, Maryland 20852. This clearinghouse disseminates information important in family planning, such as the information services
bulletin, *Adolescent Pregnancy, Early Childbearing, and Parenthood.*

Office of Adolescent Pregnancy Programs. Room 725H, Hubert H.
Humphrey Building, 200 Independence Avenue, N.W., Washington,
D.C. 20201. Funds federal studies demonstrating research on adolescent
pregnancy and parenting.

Planned Parenthood Federation of America. 810 Seventh Avenue, New

York, New York 10019. This is a national organization with chapters in many cities. Its major services include pregnancy-related counseling, education services, workshops on family planning, and contraceptive and abortion clinics.

Population Institute. 110 Maryland Avenue, N.E., Washington, D.C. 20002. Concerned with bringing the world's population into balance with its resources and environment, creating population stability, and enhancing the quality of life.

Support Center for School-Based Clinics. Suite 148, 5650 Kirby, Houston, Texas 77005 and Suite 1200, 1012 Fourteenth Street, N.W., Washington, D.C. 20005. A national resource to provide technical assistance, publications, and an annual conference to established and emerging sites across the country.

U.S. Department of Health and Human Services. Public Health Services, Health Services Administration, Bureau of Community Health Services, Rockville, Maryland 20857.

Professional Organizations

American Public Health Association. 1015 Fifteenth Street, N.W., Washington, D.C. 20005. The Population and Family Planning Section of this organization covers a wide range of disciplines and professions concerned with issues of population and family planning in the United States and throughout the world. These concerns include family planning, sexuality education, contraceptive advertising, international family planning, male involvement, and abortion.

Association for the Care of Children's Health. 3615 Wisconsin Avenue, N.W., Washington, D.C. 20016. Formerly the Association for the Care of Children in Hospitals, this organization is committed to humanizing health care for children, adolescents, and their families.

Child Welfare League of America. 67 Irving Place, New York, New York 10003. Concerned with any facet of social policy, including adolescent pregnancy, that bears on the welfare of youth and their families. Its membership is composed of professionals who work for child and family welfare through administration, supervision, casework, group work, community organization, teaching, or research.

National Association of Social Workers. 2 Park Avenue, New York, New York 10016. NASW is composed of caseworkers in the field of social welfare, many of whom work with teenage parents.

National Council on Family Relations. 1910 West County Road B., Suite 147, Saint Paul, Minnesota 55113. NCFR is dedicated to furthering all aspects of family life in terms of program development, education, and research. Teenage pregnancy has been an ongoing concern of the organization.

National Family Life Education Network. ETR Associates, 1700 Mission Street, Suite 203, Santa Cruz, California 95060. Disseminates family life materials and helps promote and develop responsive and responsible programs in family life and sex education.

Periodicals

This section highlights the major periodicals in the field that publish articles pertaining to adolescent pregnancy prevention, sexuality, and parenthood. The periodicals list is classified into three types: professional journals, popular magazines, and newsletters. Professional journals are usually, but not always, sponsored by a professional organization and refereed by experts in the field; their content tends to be academic and research based in nature. Popular magazines are generally written for the layperson in a casual style and their articles sometimes lack a sound scientific basis. Nevertheless, many of the magazines listed here publish articles by top experts in the field. Newsletters are published by assistance organizations that keep readers abreast of recent happenings in the field.

Professional Journals

Adolescence. Libra Publishers, Inc., 4901 Morena Blvd., Suite 207, San Diego, California 92117. An international quarterly devoted to coordination of the problems of adolescents among the various disciplines: psychiatry, psychology, physiology, sociology, and education.

American Journal of Public Health. American Public Health Association, 1015 Fifteenth Street, N.W., Washington, D.C. 20005. Published by the American Public Health Association, this monthly journal contains provocative commentary on current topics, articles on critical health issues, public health briefs, and book reviews.

Child Development. SACD, 570 Ellis Avenue, Chicago, Illinois 60637. A research journal citing findings on all aspects of development including adolescence. Published by the University of Chicago Press and sponsored by the Society for Research in Child Development.

Child Study Journal. State University College of New York at Buffalo, 1300 Elmwood Avenue, Buffalo, New York 14222. Publishes theory and research on child and adolescent development. Particular attention is given to articles devoted to the educational and psychological aspects of development. Published by the Faculty of Applied and Professional Studies, State University of New York at Buffalo.

Child Welfare. Child Welfare League of America, Inc., 67 Irving Place, New York, New York 10003. Extends knowledge in any youth welfare or related service on any aspect of administration, supervision, casework, group work, community organization, teaching research, interpretation, or any facet of interdisciplinary approaches to the field or on issues of social policy that bear on the welfare of children and families. Sponsored by the Child Welfare League of America, Inc.

Children Today. Room 356-G, 200 Independence Avenue, S.W., Washington, D.C. 20201. Deals with social problems, social policy, and government-related services and issues and child care. Published by the Office of Human Development Services, Department of Health and Human Services.

Developmental Psychology. American Psychological Association, 1200 Seventeenth Street, N.W., Washington, D.C. 20036. Publishes articles that advance knowledge and theory about human development across the lifespan.

Family Perspective. 822 SWKT, Brigham Young University, Provo, Utah 84602. A multidisciplinary journal which seeks articles, reports, and essays on any aspect of family life. The overall objective is to disseminate information that may be used by teachers and family-life educators as well as by concerned others.

Family Planning Perspectives. The Alan Guttmacher Institute, 111 Fifth Avenue, New York, New York 10003. This bimonthly journal of The Alan Guttmacher Institute serves the interdisciplinary reproductive health care field and publishes findings from the latest surveys and research in family planning.

Family Relations. National Council on Family Relations, 1910 West County Road B, Suite 147, St. Paul, Minnesota 55113. Directed toward practitioners serving the family field through education, counseling, and community services. It disseminates reports of experiences in these areas, provides leads for others to explore, evaluates work using innovative methods, and discusses the application of research and theory to practice.

Journal of Adolescent Health Care. Elsevier Science Publishing Company, 52 Vanderbilt Avenue, New York, New York 10017. The official journal of the Society of Adolescent Medicine is committed to the understanding of adolescence and the delivery of optimal comprehensive health care to youth. The journal addresses all professions that focus on preventive medical problems and health care needs of youth.

Journal of Marriage and Family. National Council on Family Relations, 1910 West County Road B, Suite 147, St. Paul, Minnesota 55113. A quarterly journal for the presentation of original theory, research interpretation, and critical discussion of materials related to marriage and the family.

Journal of School Health. American School Health Association, 1521 S. Water Street, P.O. Box 708, Kent, Ohio 44240. The official journal of the American School Health Association that publishes articles on topics relating to or affecting health promotion and health instruction in the schools.

Journal of Sex Research. Department of Psychology, Syracuse University, Syracuse, New York 13210. Serves as a forum for the interdisciplinary exchange of knowledge among professionals concerned with the scientific study of sex.

Journal of Youth and Adolescence. Plenum Publishing Corporation, 233 Spring Street, New York, New York 10013. This multidisciplinary journal publishes papers based on experimental evidence and data, theoretical papers, comprehensive review articles, and clinical reports of relevance to the subject of youth and adolescence.

Parenting Studies. Department of Child Development, Iowa State University, Ames, Iowa 50011. An international, quarterly journal that publishes articles on issues of parenting including research on teenage parenting, case studies, reports on innovative programs, and models and commentaries on trends in parenting.

Pediatric Nursing. Anthony J. Jannetti, Inc., North Woodbury Road, Box 56, Pitman, New Jersey 08071. Publishes articles that reflect trends, policies, practice, and research in pediatric nursing. Topics are timely and cover areas of adolescent sexuality, contraception, and fatherhood.

Social Work. Editorial Office, NASW, 2 Park Avenue, New York, New York 10016. Publishes articles that have implications for social workers and other practitioners.

Youth and Society. Sage Publications, 2111 West Hillcrest Drive, Newbury Park, California 91320. An interdisciplinary journal directed at the dissemination of theoretical and empirical knowledge on child and youth socialization. The focus is especially on implications and consequences of findings for social policy, program development, and institutional functioning.

Magazines

The Family Life Educator. National Family Life Education Network, ETR Associates, 1700 Mission Street, Suite 203, Santa Cruz, California 95061. A quarterly magazine for senior high students and their parents to promote teen ability to discuss attitudes related to the roles of various family members. It teaches about family life and sexuality and can be used in schools or in the home.

The Early Adolescence Magazine. T.E.A.M. Associates, Inc., P.O. Box 1167, Clarksville, Maryland 21029. A bimonthly magazine focusing on children of middle school or junior high school age. It provides a forum for health care workers, lawyers, educators, and others interested in adolescents.

Newsletters

Carnegie Quarterly. Carnegie Corporation of New York, 437 Madison Avenue, New York, New York 10022. A newsletter describing activities supported by the corporation, many of which deal with adolescent pregnancy.

Center for Early Adolescence Newsletter. Center for Early Adolescence, Suite 223, Car Mill Mall, Carroboro, North Carolina 27510. Contains valuable resources for professionals who work with children between 10 and 15 years old. Quarterly.

CDF Reports. Children's Defense Fund, 122 C Street, N.W., Washington, D.C. 20001. The monthly newsletter of the Children's Defense Fund reports news and issues on children and adolescents.

Clinic News. Center for Population Options, 1012 14th Street, N.W., Suite 1200, Washington, D.C. 20005. A quarterly newsletter that reports on up-to-date information on the school-based clinic movement. Articles on new resources, program developments, and legislation.

Family Resource Coalition Report. 230 North Michigan Avenue, Suite 1625, Chicago, Illinois 60601. Published three times a year, the report contains an exchange of ideas about families: model program descriptions, thought-provoking dialogues, reviews of outstanding work by organizations and individuals, discussions of legislative and policy perspectives, and strategies for raising funds and evaluating programs.

Male Involvement Bulletin. Center for Population Options, 1012 14th Street, N.W., Suite 1200, Washington, D.C. 20005. Provides the missing ingredient of the male's involvement in family planning.

Network Report. National Family Life Education Network, 1700 Mission Street, Suite 203, Santa Cruz, California 95060. Provides information on family life projects, research, materials, laws, and public policy from the perspectives of home, church, school, and community.

Teenage Parents/Western Regional Educational Committee Newsletter. Jeanne Lindsay, Editor, 6595 San Haroldo Way, Buena Park, California 90620.

Audiovisuals

This section includes the burgeoning numbers of audiovisuals on adolescent pregnancy prevention, particularly as it relates to teenage fathers. These resources are arranged by type of audiovisual.

16MM Films

Boys and Girls Together. Explores teenage sexual behavior and attitudes, peer pressure, teenage pregnancy, and parental attitudes toward teenage sexuality and sex education. The Media Guild, P.O. Box 811, Solana Beach, California 92075. 28 minutes. 1981.

If You Want to Dance. An unwed teenage boy and girl are faced with an unplanned pregnancy. The film shows that the dilemma is not just the girl's but that boys share it. New Dimension Films, 85895 Lorane Highway, Eugene, Oregon 97405. 14 minutes, color. 1981.

Teenage Fathers. This Academy Award-winning film presents interviews with real-life teenage males whose girlfriends have become pregnant. Provides a balanced account of the problems and traumas arising from such an experience. Covers the various options, legal rights, and lack of rights of young people in this predicament. Children's Home Society of California,

5429 McConnell Avenue, Los Angeles, California 90069. 16 minutes, color. 1978.

The Teenage Pregnancy Experience. This film is designed to prepare expectant teenage parents for birth and parenthood; to discuss options for pregnant adolescents; to promote discussion on pregnancy; and to depict realistic situations for use with teen groups as well as in professional training. Parenting Pictures, 121 N.W. Crystal Street, Crystal River, Florida 32629. 28 minutes, color. 1982.

Wayne's Decision. This film dramatizes in realistic dialogue the crisis of becoming an adolescent father. It helps viewers recognize the tragic fact that there is no single solution to teenage pregnancy. Memphis Association for Planned Parenthood (MAP), 1407 Union Avenue, Memphis, Tennessee 38104. 6 minutes. 1980.

Filmstrips

Do I Want to Be a Parent? Now? Ever? Debates the emotional and intellectual pros and cons of becoming a parent in today's society, stressing that personal choice is the key issue. Sunburst Communications, 39 Washington Avenue, Pleasantville, New York 10570-9971.

Four Pregnant Teenagers: Four Different Decisions. These true-to-life vignettes dramatize the difficult decisions faced by unwed pregnant teenagers. This program forces students to weigh the emotional, ethical, and financial problems involved in the four options available to pregnant teens: adoption, marriage, single parenthood, and abortion. Also available on videocassette. Sunburst Communications, 39 Washington Avenue, Pleasantville, New York 10570-9971.

His Baby, Too: Problems of Teenage Pregnancy. This group of filmstrips, titled *Dave's Story, The Choices,* and *Making the Decision,* examines the feelings of teenage fathers and argues against the stereotype that portrays him as an aggressive lover who unfeelingly leaves his sex partner. It also examines the often overlooked emotional feelings of adolescent fathers, regarding issues on abortion and the role of the father in the child's upbringing. Sunburst Communications, 39 Washington Avenue, Pleasantville, New York 10570-9971. Three sound filmstrips, 38 minutes. 1980.

Pregnancy: A Teenage Epidemic. This filmstrip presents the statistics on adolescent pregnancy, what these numbers mean for us as a society, and what can be done to reduce the epidemic. Current Affairs Films, P.O. Box 398, 24 Danbury Road, Wilton, Connecticut 06880. 16 minutes. 1978.

Teenage Sex: How to Say No. This set of three filmstrips was designed especially for adolescents who need guidance in resisting pressure to be sexually active. Also available on videocassette. Sunburst Communications, 39 Washington Avenue, Pleasantville, New York 10570-9971.

Videotapes

It Only Takes Once. Dealing with adolescent pregnancy prevention, this video is presented by teenagers on the realities of sex and the issue of pregnancy. Includes group discussions with a high school sexuality class about the feelings and pressures that accompany adolescent sexual experiences. Intermedia Inc., 1600 Dexter Avenue North, Seattle, Washington, 98109. 20 minutes. 1987.

Me, A Teen Father? This videotape conveys the guilt and anguish over teenage fatherhood and recreates a 17-year-old boy's romance ending in pregnancy. Provides insight into the fears and feelings of adolescent fathers and demonstrates the depth of emotions that teens often experience. Centron Films (CEN), 1621 West 9th, Lawrence, Kansas 66044. 13 minutes. 1980. Also available in 16 mm film.

Teens Having Babies. This film shows a teenage couple having their baby in a supportive hospital atmosphere. It also shows teens getting prenatal care, including medical history and pelvic exam. Polymorph Films, 118 South Street, Boston, Massachusetts 02111. 20 minutes, color. Also available in 16mm film.

What Guys Want. Teenagers of diverse ethnic, racial, and economic backgrounds express their attitudes and feelings about maleness and their male sexual behavior in a candid and compelling manner. It examines values and helps teens of both sexes understand the consequences of sexual behavior and delaying sexual activity. Polymorph Films, 118 South Street, Boston, Massachusetts 02111. 16 minutes, color. Also available in 16mm film.

Programs for Teenage Fathers

Programs for teenage fathers continue to develop throughout the United States. Individuals, organizations, and advocacy groups work together to muster community resources to help bridge the ever-increasing gaps between needs and services. Some selected programs and addresses of existing programs are included in this section. This list of models represents a selected

variety of collaborative efforts among various groups and is not intended to
be all inclusive.

Athletes Coaching Teens (ACT 1)
Dr. Steven Danish
Department of Psychology
Virginia Commonwealth University
Richmond, Virginia

The Fatherhood Program
Face to Face Health and
    Counseling Services
736 Mendota Street
St. Paul, Minnesota 55102

The Fatherhood Project
Teen Parent Program
2041 N.W. Everett
Portland, Oregon 97209

Fathers' Outreach Program
Teen Parents' Program
YWCA of Dutchess County
18 Bancroft Road
Poughkeepsie, New York 12601

Fifth Ward Enrichment Program
1700 Gregg Street
Houston, Texas 77020

Foster Grandparent Program
9851 Hamilton
Detroit, Michigan 48202

Male Adolescent Program
Adolescent Family Center
Rush-Presbyterian-St. Lukes
1725 West Harrison, Suite 436
Chicago, Illinois 60612

Male Involvement Program
Planned Parenthood
425 South Cherry Street, S.E.
Grand Rapids, Michigan 49503

The Male's Place
Mecklenburg County Health Dept.
Beatties Ford Road
Charlotte, N.C. 28206

Project Alpha
Alpha Phi Alpha Fraternity
4432 Martin Luther King Jr. Drive
Chicago, Illinois 60653

Project MARCH
Planned Parenthood
1200 Sansom Street
Philadelphia, Penn. 19107

Teen Father Collaboration
Bank Street College of Education
610 West 112 Street
New York, New York 10025

The Teen Father Program
Hough-Norwood Youth Services
8555 Hough Avenue
Cleveland, Ohio 44106

Teen Fatherhood Project
YMCA of Greater Bridgeport
651 State Street
Bridgeport, Conn. 06604

Teen Fathers' Program
Department of Pediatrics
Medical College of Pennsylvania
    Hospital
3300 Henry Avenue
Philadelphia, Penn. 19129

Teen Indian Father Project
3045 Park Avenue
Minneapolis, Minnesota 55407

Teenage Father Program (TAPP)
Jefferson County Public Schools
1100 Sylvia Street
Louisville, Kentucky 40217

Teenage Pregnancy and Parenting
Fatherhood Project
995 Potrero Avenue
Ward 80N
San Francisco, California 94110

Young Men's Clinic
Columbia Presbyterian Hospital
Columbia University
60 Haven Avenue
New York, New York 10032

Young Men's Sexuality Awareness
  Program
Norfolk Area Health
  Education Center
930 Majestic Avenue
Suite 220
Norfolk, Virginia 23504

Professional Library

This section provides an extensive bibliography of further readings for professionals in the field who wish to pursue their study in more detail. The bibliography that follows is drawn from professional journals and is subdivided into four interest groups: researchers; program developers and policymakers; health and human services practitioners; and general public.

Researchers

Barret, R.L., & Robinson, B.E. (1982) A descriptive study of teenage expectant fathers. *Family Relations* 31:349–52.

Brown, S.V. (1983) The commitment and concerns of black adolescent parents. *Social Work Research & Abstracts* 19:27–34.

Card, J.J., & Wise, L.L. (1978) Teenage mothers and teenage fathers: The impact of early childbearing on the parents' personal and professional lives. *Family Planning Perspectives* 16:77–82.

Clark, S.D., Zabin, L.S., & Hardy, J.B. (1984) Sex, contraception, and parenthood: Experience and attitudes among urban black young men. *Family Planning Perspectives* 16:77–82.

de Lissovoy, V. (1973a) Child care by adolescent parents. *Children Today* 2:22–25.

de Lissovoy, V. (1973b) High school marriages: A longitudinal study. *Journal of Marriage and the Family* 35:245–55.

Earls, F., & Siegel, B. (1980) Precocious fathers. *American Journal of Orthopsychiatry* 50:469–80.

Elster, A., & Lamb, M. (1982) Adolescent fathers: A group potentially at risk for parenting failure. *Infant Mental Health Journal* 3:148–55.

Elster, A.B., & Panzarine, S. (1983) Teenage fathers: Stresses during gestation and early parenthood. *Clinical Pediatrics* 22:700–703.

Fry, P.S. (1983) Teenage fathers: An exploration of their developmental needs and anxieties and the implications for clinical-social intervention and services. *Journal of Psychiatric Treatment & Evaluation* 5:219–27.

Furstenberg, F.F. (1980) Children's names and paternal claims: Bonds between unmarried fathers and their children. *Journal of Family Issues* 1:31–57.

Gershenson, H.P. (1983) Redefining fatherhood in families with white adolescent mothers. *Journal of Marriage and the Family* 45:591–99.

Hendricks, L.E. (1980) Unwed adolescent fathers: Problems they face and their sources of social support. *Adolescence* 15:862–69.

Hendricks, L.E. (1982) Unmarried black adolescent fathers' attitudes toward abortion, contraception, and sexuality: A preliminary report. *Journal of Adolescent Health Care* 2:119–203.

Hendricks, L.E., Howard, C.S., & Caesar, P.P. (1981a) Black unwed adolescent fathers: A comparative study of their problems and help-seeking behavior. *Journal of the National Medical Association* 73:863–68.

Hendricks, L.E., Howard, C.S., & Caesar, P.P. (1981b) Help-seeking behavior among select populations of black unmarried adolescent fathers: Implications for human service agencies. *American Journal of Public Health* 7:733–35.

Hendricks, L.E., & Montgomery, T. (1983) A limited population of unmarried adolescent fathers: A preliminary report of their views on fatherhood and the relationship with the mothers of their children. *Adolescence* 18:201–10.

Hendricks, L.E., Montgomery, T.A., Fullilove, R. (1984) Educational achievement and locus of control among black adolescent fathers. *Journal of Negro Education* 53:182–88.

Kerchoff, A.C., & Parrow, A.A. (1979) The effect of early marriage on the educational attainment of young men. *Journal of Marriage and the Family* 41:97–107.

Lamb, M.E., & Elster, A.B. (1985) Adolescent mother-infant-father relationships. *Developmental Psychology* 21:768–73.

Lerman, R.I. (1986) Who are the young absent fathers? *Youth and Society* 18:3–27.

Lorenzi, M.E., Klerman, L.V., & Jekel, J.F. (1977) School-age parents: How permanent a relationship? *Adolescence* 12:45–57.

McCoy, J.E., & Tyler, F.B. (1985) Selected psychosocial characteristics of black unwed adolescent fathers. *Journal of Adolescent Health Care* 6:12–16.

McHenry, P.C., Walters, L.H., & Johnson, C. (1979) Adolescent pregnancy: A review of literature. *The Family Coordinator* 28:17–28.

Montmayor, A.Q. (1983) Parents and adolescents in conflict: All families some of the time; some families all of the time. *Journal of Early Adolescence* 3:83–102.

Nakashima, I.I., & Camp, B.W. (1984) Fathers of infants born to adolescent mothers. *American Journal of Diseases of Children* 138:452–54.

Nettleton, C.A., & Cline, D.W. (1975) Dating patterns, sexual relationships and use of contraceptives of 700 unwed mothers during a two-year period following delivery. *Adolescence* 10:45–57.

Panzarine, S.A., & Elster, A.B. (1983) Coping in a group of expectant adolescent fathers: An exploratory study. *Journal of Adolescent Health Care* 4:117–20.

Parke, R.D., Power, T.G., & Fisher, T. (1980) The adolescent father's impact on the mother and child. *Journal of Social Issues* 36:88–106.

Pauker, J.D. (1971) Fathers of children conceived out of wedlock: Pregnancy, high school, psychological test results. *Developmental Psychology* 4:215–18.

Pfuhl, E.H. (1978) The unwed father: A non-deviant rule breaker. *Sociological Quarterly* 19:113–28.

Redmond, M.A. (1985) Attitudes of adolescent males toward adolescent pregnancy and fatherhood. *Family Relations* 34:337–42.

Rivara, F.P., Sweeney, P.J., & Henderson, B.F. (1985) A study of low socioeconomic status, black teenage fathers and their nonfather peers. *Pediatrics* 75:648–56.

Rivara, F.P., Sweeney, P.J., & Henderson, B.F. (1986) Black teenage fathers: What happens when the child is born? *Pediatrics* 78:151–58.

Robbins, M.M., & Lynn, D. (1973, November) The unwed fathers: Generation, recidivism and attitudes about intercourse in California Youth Authority Wards. *Journal of Sex Research* 9:334–41.

Robinson, B.E., & Barret, R.L. (1982) Issues and problems related to the research on teenage fathers: A critical analysis. *Journal of School Health* 52:596–600.

Robinson, B.E., & Barret, R.L. (1987) Self-concept and anxiety of adolescent and adult fathers. *Adolescence.* In press.

Robinson, B.E., Barret, R.L., & Skeen, P. (1983) Locus of control of unwed adolescent fathers versus adolescent nonfathers. *Perceptual and Motor Skills* 56:397–98.

Rothstein, A.A. (1978) Adolescent males, fatherhood, and abortion. *Journal of Youth and Adolescence* 7:203–14.

Russ-Eft, D., Sprenger, M., & Beever, H. (1979) Antecedents of adolescent parenthood and consequences at age 30. *The Family Coordinator* 28:173–79.

Russell, E.S. (1980) Unscheduled parenthood: Transition to parent for the teenager. *Journal of Social Issues* 36:45–63.

Sawin, D.B., & Parke, R.D. (1976) Adolescent fathers: Some implications from recent research on parental roles. *Educational Horizons* 55:38–43.

Vaz, R., Smolen, P., & Miller, C. (1983) Adolescent pregnancy: Involvement of the male partner. *Journal of Adolescent Health Care* 4:246–50.

Vincent, C. (1960) The unmarried fathers and the mores: Sexual exploiter as an ex post facto label. *American Sociological Review* 25:40–46.

Westney, O.E., Cole, O.J., & Munford, T.L. (1986) Adolescent unwed prospective fathers: Readiness for fatherhood and behaviors toward the mother and the expected infant. *Adolescence* 21:901–11.

Program Developers/Policymakers

Abernathy, V. (1976) Prevention of unwanted pregnancy among teenagers. *Primary Care* 3:399–406.

Apte, D.V. (1987) A plan to prevent adolescent pregnancy and reduce infant mortality. *Public Health Reports* 102:80–86.

Bell, C.A., Casto, G., & Daniels, D.S. (1983) Ameliorating the impact of teen-age pregnancy on parent and child. *Child Welfare* 62:167–73.

Black, C., & DeBlassie, R.R. (1985) Adolescent pregnancy: Contributing factors, consequences, treatment, and plausible solutions. *Adolescence* 20:283–90.

Flick, L.H. (1986) Paths to adolescent parenthood: Implications for prevention. *Public Health Reports* 101:132–47.

Goldstein, H., & Wallace, H.M. (1976) Services for and needs of pregnant teenagers in large cities of the U.S., 1976. *Public Health Report* 93:46–54.

Johnson, L.B., & Staples, R.E. (1979) Family planning and the young minority male: A pilot project. *The Family Coordinator* 28:535–43.

Johnson, S. (15 March 1978) Two pioneer programs help unwed teenage fathers cope. *The New York Times*, 54.

Knowles, G.A., & Tripple, P.A. (1986) Cyesis program addresses teenage pregnancy and family well-being. *Journal of Home Economics* 78:25–28.

Lyons, D.J. (1968) Developing a program for pregnant teenagers through the cooperation of school, health department and federal agencies. *American Journal of Public Health* 58:2225–30.

McMurray, G.L. (1968) Project Teen Aid: A community action approach to services for pregnant unmarried teenagers. *American Journal of Public Health* 58:1848–53.

Moore, K.A. (1978) Teenage childbirth and welfare dependency. *Family Planning Perspectives* 10:233–35.

Nakashima, I.I. (1978) Teenage pregnancy—its causes, costs and consequences. *Nurse Practitioner* 3:10–13.

Zabin, L.S., Hirsch, M.B., Smith, E.A., Streett, R., & Hardy, J.B. (1986) Evaluation of a pregnancy prevention program for urban teenagers. *Family Planning Perspectives* 18:119–26.

Health and Human Services Practitioners

Allen-Meares, P. (1984) Adolescent pregnancy and parenting: The forgotten adolescent father and his parents. *Journal of Social Work & Human Sexuality* 3:27–38.

Barret, R.L., & Robinson, B.E. (1981) Teenage fathers: A profile. *Personnel and Guidance Journal* 60:226–28.

Barret, R.L., & Robinson, B.E. (1982) Teenage fathers: Neglected too long. *Social Work* 27:484–88.

Barret, R.L., & Robinson, B.E. (1986, July/August) Adolescent fathers: The other half of teenage pregnancy. *Pediatric Nursing* 12:273–77.

Brown, S.V. (1984) The commitment and concerns of black adolescent parents. *Social Work Research and Abstracts* 19:27–34.

Carparulo, F., London, K. (1981) Adolescent fathers: Adolescents first, fathers second. *Issues in Health Care of Women* 3:23–33.

Elster, A.B., & Panzarine, S.A. (1979) Adolescent pregnancy—where is the unwed teenage father? *Pediatrics,* 63:824.

Elster, A.B., & Panzarine, S. (1980) Unwed teenager fathers: Emotional and health educational needs. *Journal of Adolescent Health Care* 1:116–20.

Finkel, M., & Finkel, D. (1975) Sexual and contraceptive knowledge, attitudes and behavior of male adolescents. *Family Planning Perspectives* 7:257–60.

Foster, C.D., & Miller, G.M. Adolescent pregnancy: A challenge for counselors. *Personnel and Guidance Journal* 59:236–40.

Gebbhart, G.O., & Wolff, J.R. (1977) The unwed pregnant adolescent and her male partner. *The Journal of Reproductive Medicine* 19:137–40.

Goodwin, N.J. (1987) Black adolescent pregnancy: A special issue. *Journal of Community Health*. Based on a symposium sponsored by the Empire State Medical Association, the twelve articles in this issue address the problem of adolescent pregnancy in America.

Hendricks, L.E. (1983) Suggestions for reaching unmarried black adolescent fathers. *Child Welfare* 62:141–46.

Kahn, J.S., & Elster, A.B. (1983) Adolescent fathers—Can they be reached? *Journal of Adolescent Health Care* 4:215.

Panzarine, S., & Elster, A. (1982) Prospective adolescent fathers: Stresses during pregnancy and implications for nursing interventions. *Journal of Psychosocial Nursing and Mental Health Services* 20:21–24.

Pierce, A.D. (1981) Adoption policy and the "unwed father": An exploratory study of social worker response to changing conceptions of father-hood. *Dissertation Abstracts International* 42:387A.

Rivara, F.P. (1981) Teenage pregnancy: The forgotten father. *Developmental Behavioral Pediatrics* 2:142–46.

Rivera-Casale, C., Klerman, L.V., Manela, R. (1984) The relevance of child-support enforcement to school-age parents. *Child Welfare* 63:521–32.

Sadler, L.S., & Catrone, C. (1983) The adolescent parent: A dual developmental crisis. *Journal of Adolescent Health Care* 4:100–105.

Scales, P. (1977, July) Males and morals: Teenage contraceptive behavior amid the double standard. *The Family Coordinator:* 211–22.

Sheehan, M.K., Ostwald, S.K., & Rothenberger, J. (1986) Perceptions of sexual responsibility: Do young men and women agree? *Pediatric Nursing* 12:17–21.

Vadies, E., & Hale, D. (1979) Adolescent males: Attitudes towards abortion, contraception, and sexuality. *Advances in Planned Parenthood* 13:35–41.

Vaz, R., Sole, P., & Miller, C. (1983) Adolescent pregnancy. *Journal of Adolescent Health Care* 4:246–50.

General Public

Cantarone, E. (1985) Children who have babies. *Women's Day* (February): 100, 101, 152, 154.

Connolly, L. (1978) Boy fathers. *Human Behavior* (January): 40–43.

Robinson, B.E., & Barret, R.L. (1985, December). Teenage fathers. *Psychology Today* 19:66–70.

Stark, E. (1986, October) Young, innocent and pregnant. *Psychology Today* 20:28–35.

Stengel, R. (9 December 1985) The missing father myth. *Time:*90.

Van Biema, D. (13 April 1987) What you don't know about teen sex. *People Magazine* 27:110–21.

Index

Abortion, 134; attitudes toward, 62, 67; and blacks, 9; father's participation in decision, 58, 108, 109
ACE Psychological and Cooperative English Test, 76
ACT 1 Program, 130
Adams, M.L., 135
Adolescent Life Programs, 13
Adoption, teenage father's rights, 25, 108, 109, 127
Adult fathers and teenage fathers, 65–67, 85, 120–121
Age, 120–121; and contraceptive use, 3, 4, 120; and fatherhood, effects of, 65–67; and first intercourse, 2–3, 26–28, 120; vs. mother's age, 8; and pregnancy risk, 4; as research variable, 83–84
Aid to Families with Dependent Children, 41
AIDS, xi, 4, 11, 112
Alan Guttmacher Institute, 2, 3, 6, 27, 28, 43, 140
Alcohol abuse, 48, 61
Allen-Meares, Paula, 5, 40, 74, 82, 109, 115, 119, 125, 127
Alpha Phi Alpha Fraternity, 130
American Journal of Orthopsychiatry, 72
Ann Arbor, Mich., 126
Anxiety, 66, 67
Arians, Bruce, 130
Arizona, 137–138
Audiovisual resources, 156–158

Babikian, H.M., 60, 72
Baldwin, W., 45

Baltimore, Md., 6, 139
Bank Street College of Education, 42, 128, 137
Banks, Richard, 32
Barret, Robert L., 6, 10, 22, 27, 30, 32, 47, 55, 57, 61, 63, 64, 66, 72, 73, 74, 83, 92, 93, 103, 109, 110, 118
Beever, H., 27, 41, 76, 77
Belsky, J., 47–48, 81, 92
Big Stone Gap Public School System, Va., 30
Birth, father's presence during, 32, 128
Birth control. *See* Contraceptives
Birth defects and teenage parents, 44, 46
Black, C., 113, 120
Blacks, x, 76; and abortion, 9; attitudes toward child and mother, 29; and contraceptives, 4; incidence of teenage pregnancy, 9; and marriage, 9; and prevention programs, 130–131, 133; and research, 81, 84
Blythe, B.J., 138
Bolton, F.G., 47–48, 127
Books, 117, 143–149
Bowen, Otis R., 39
Bozett, F., 72
Bridgeport, Conn., 128–129
Bronfenbrenner, Urie, 111
Brooks-Gunn, J., 127
Brown, Shirley V., 8, 27, 28, 29, 31, 78, 127

Caesar, P.O., 27, 108, 119
Cain, V.S., 45

ness, 137–138; as research source, 73–74, 81; social network, 47
Mott, F.L., 6, 137, 138–139
Mueller, J., 74
Munford, T.L., 8, 27, 29, 31, 32
Muskegan, Mich., 139
Myths about teenage fathers. *See* Stereotypes of teenage father

Nakashima, I.I., 8, 42, 43, 65–66, 67, 76, 121
Name of child and father, 42, 43–44, 74
Namerow, P.B., 4, 120
National Center for Health Statistics, 9
National Longitudinal Survey, 76
National Longitudinal Survey of Work Experience of Youth, 6, 41
Native Americans, 133
Natural childbirth classes, 128
Needle, R.H., 3
Netherlands, teenage pregnancy rate, 2
Nettleton, Calif., 27, 42
Neurotic personality, teenage father as, 24–25
New York City, 4, 128, 136
Newsletters, 155–156
Nickel, P.S., 136
Nonfathers and teenage fathers, 29, 50, 61–64, 67; and research, 77–78, 84
Norfolk Area Health Education Clinic, 132
Notter Internal-External Locus of Control Scale, 64
Nowicki-Strickland Locus of Control Scale, 64
Number of children and teenage father, 41
Number of teenage fathers, 8–9
Nye, F.I., 27, 42, 44

Oates, R.K., 46
Ostwald, S.K., 4, 113
Out of Wedlock (Young), 24

Pannor, R., 8, 24–25, 31, 32, 61, 75, 76

Panzarine, S., 7, 8, 9, 27, 29, 32, 40, 55, 57, 59, 60, 76, 83, 84, 85, 119, 127
Parents of father and mother, 7–8, 113; attitudes toward teenage pregnancy, 7–8; hostility from, 60; programs for, 129–130; as role model, 60–61; support from, 115
Parke, R.D., 110
Parrow, A.A., 27, 41
Pauker, Jerome D., 29, 53, 55, 63, 64, 73
Peacock, Ernie, 127
Peer groups: isolation from, 55, 56, 57, 61, 67; support from, 115–117, 130–131
Periodicals, 117, 152–156
Personal Attribute Inventory, 66
Personal fable, 5
Pfuhl, E.H., 75
Phantom Father myth of teenage father, 22, 31–32
Philadelphia, Pa., 127, 128, 133
Philliber, S.G., 4, 120
Phipps-Yonas, S., 27
Pierce, A.D., 109, 127
Pittman, K., 135, 136
Platts, H.K., 8, 73
Portland, Oreg., 128
Poughkeepsie, N.Y., 128, 129
Power, T.G., 110
Pregnancy, father's involvement with, 32, 110; *see also* Birth, father's presence during
Premarital sex, incidence of, 9
Premature births, 39, 44
Prevention programs, x–xi, 11–13, 111–113, 126–127; evaluation of, 138–139; model, 130–136; *see also* Counseling; Sex education
Professional journals, 152–155
Professional organizations, 151–152
Programs, 125–140, 163–164; evaluation of, 137–140; lists of, 158–160; *see also* Intervention programs; Prevention programs
Project Alpha, 130–131
Project MARCH, 127, 130, 133
Project Talent, 40–41, 77

About the Author

Bryan Robinson is professor of child and family development at the University of North Carolina at Charlotte. He is coauthor of three other books, *Child Development and Relationships,* *The Developing Father,* and *Latchkey Kids* (also with Lexington Books) and has published more than fifty articles in professional journals and such popular magazines as *Psychology Today.* Dr. Robinson has written scripts for national television programs on child development and has appeared on national radio and television discussing his original research on teenage fathers, with whom he has worked for eight years. He also has spoken at national and international professional health care meetings on the topic.